Oxford Music Books for Schools
Foundation Course

Jack Dobbs, Roger Fiske, and Michael Lane

Ears
and
Eyes

Teacher's Book

Music Department
OXFORD UNIVERSITY PRESS
44 CONDUIT STREET, LONDON WᵢR oDE

Acknowledgements are due to the following for permission to reproduce songs or poems:

Chapter 9: Novello & Co. Ltd. ('The Spinning Song' from *Second Tunes for Recorder and Piano* (Anne Mendoza), 'Mr. Rabbit' (melody), 'Venezuelan Carol', 'Go and tell Aunt Nancy', 'The Little Pig', 'Donald, O Donald' (words), 'The Swapping Song'); Cambridge University Press ('Down by the Crystal Fountain' from *Something to Sing* Book 1); Harvard University Press ('Mr. Rabbit' (words) from *On the Trail of the Negro* (Dorothy Scarborough) © 1925 by Harvard University Press, 1953 by Mary McDaniel Parker); Faber Music Ltd. on behalf of J. Curwen & Sons Ltd. ('The Baby King', 'Blow away the morning dew', 'This Old Man', 'Billy Boy'); G. Schirmer, 140 Strand, London WC2R 1HH ('Abiyoyo'); The Agent to the Cecil Sharp Estate ('Sing, said the Mother', 'Mocking Bird'); Ginn and Company ('Nine Red Horsemen', 'Pirulito'); William Heinemann Ltd. ('Cats' (Francis Scarfe) from *Underworlds*); E. J. Arnold & Son Ltd. ('The Donkey's Burial'); David Higham Associates ('Cottage' (Eleanor Farjeon) from *Then There Were Three* (Michael Joseph)); The English Folk Dance and Song Society ('Donald, O Donald' (melody)); Thomas Nelson & Sons Ltd. ('Leave her, Johnny' from *New National and Folk Song Book* Part 1 (McMahon), 'Pancakes' from *The Golden Staircase*); Nigel Nicolson ('The Greater Cats' (V. Sackville West)); Oxford University Press ('Unto us a Boy is Born', 'Rocking'), Charleton Primary School, Devon ('Goodbye, Winter').

Chapter 10: Novello & Co. Ltd. ('Soldier, Soldier', 'The Holly and the Ivy', 'The Keeper', 'John Barleycorn', 'One Man shall mow my Meadow'); The Agent to the Cecil Sharp Estate ('Bye, Bye, Baby', 'Sourwood Mountain'); Czechoslovak Theatrical and Literary Agency ('The Little Dove'); Faber Music Ltd. on behalf of J. Curwen & Sons Ltd. ('The Old Man of the Woods', 'Sweet Nightingale', 'High Germany'); Stainer & Bell Ltd ('Down to Bethlehem', 'When I first came to this Land'); The Society for Promoting Christian Knowledge ('Past Three O'Clock'); The Literary Trustees of Walter de la Mare, and the Society of Authors as their representative ('Full Moon'); The Society of Authors ('When you Walk' (James Stephens)); East Sussex County Council Education Department ('Goodbye Winter'); Mrs. C. J. A. Kunst-van Wely ('Eastertide'); J. A. Lindon ('Sink Song'); E. J. Arnold & Son Ltd. ('The Tree on the Hill'); David Higham Associates and Clive Sansom ('Dachshund' from *The Golden Unicorn* (Methuen)); Boosey & Hawkes Music Publishers Ltd. ('Time for Man Go Home' from *The Edric Connor Collection* © 1945 by Boosey & Co. Ltd.); William Heinemann Ltd. ('Slowly' (James Reeves) from *The Wandering Moon*); G. Schirmer, 140 Strand, London WC2R 1HH ('Manamolela'); Mrs. Vaughan Williams ('The Grey Hawk'); 'Sounds' from *Ounce, Dice, Trice* (Alastair Reid) published by J. M. Dent & Sons Ltd. and Littlebrown & Co.; 'Old Aunt Kate' from *American Folk Songs for Children* (Seeger) published by Doubleday & Co.; Inc. 'Hush-you-bye' from *American Ballads and Folk Songs* (John A. Lomax and Alan Lomax) published by Macmillan & Co.; Oxford University Press ('W' and 'Mrs. Button' (James Reeves) from *The Blackbird in the Lilac*, 'The Cradle', 'Hill an' Gully', 'Jumbuck Skinning Man').

ISBN 0 19 321230 7

Preface

These books are the successors of the junior series of the Oxford School Music Books. In the last twenty years or so many changes have taken place in teaching methods, and there has been a complete reappraisal of musical aims. With the arrival of new ideas there is always a danger that older ones which have proved their worth will be discarded. Not all that is old is worth preserving, but it is equally true that not all new ideas are any better. In these books we have made use of whatever seems to us to be valuable in both old and new, without following fashion for its own sake.

One important fact is that the human voice can still give pleasure to both singers and listeners; moreover there is much that can be learnt about the nature of music through the use of the voice. For this reason these books are still primarily based on songs, many of them new to the series. But singing alone cannot give children the breadth of musical experience they are capable of absorbing, and extensive use is made of the increasing range of percussion instruments that are now available, both pitched and unpitched. These often provide simple accompaniments to the songs as an alternative to the piano, and they are also used for less conventional purposes such as improvisation and small essays in composition. The suggestions for instrumental work usually spring from the songs. Similarly we have tried to show how movement and listening can be incorporated into the general scheme of work.

A new feature of the books is the tape that has been specially made to include all the listening music we have recommended. It is intended for use in conjunction with the text in the Teacher's Book. Teachers will find it more durable and easier to handle than the gramophone records from which it has been assembled.

Another new feature is the series of work cards. They are progressive in order, and they are meant to be used independently of the class as a whole, each card requiring the participation of up to four children. Their main purpose is to stimulate the child's imagination and creative ability within the area of work being done by the whole class.

In both the Pupils' Books and the work cards, pictures and poems are an important additional feature. We hope that teachers will find them useful in educating eyes as well as ears.

Books 1 and 2 are intended to provide for the musical needs of children in the lower age ranges. No precise age is specified, as standards of achievement vary from school to school. Some of the material can be adapted for the use of older children. Many teachers will find that each Pupils' Book contains enough material for one year's work, but the amount of time for music varies in different schools, and some teachers will not get through all the material. Because the books are progressive, it may be advisable in some cases to spend more than one year over each of them; the course should be taken at whatever pace suits the children best.

The preliminary chapters provide a basis of musical knowledge for the modestly endowed teacher, but we would emphasize that practical experience is more valuable than any amount of reading. Many Music Advisers run courses for teachers responsible for music, and they usually hope that those with very little musical experience will take part in order to gain confidence and widen their horizons. Those teachers who have the courage to go will find these courses very helpful, for instance over musical points which they have found difficult or obscure in print.

We would also stress the value of schools' programmes on radio and television. Though not a substitute for the classroom teacher, they are an added stimulus, often making use of resources that are not available in schools. Many of these broadcasts suggest useful follow-up activities.

Contents

Contents of Pupils' Books

BOOK ONE

BOOK TWO

1 The Scope of Music Teaching

Music, they say, is part of our national heritage, an international language, an intellectual discipline. But these are not necessarily the best reasons for teaching it. A far better reason is that making music can give so much sheer pleasure. This pleasure can arise both from individual effort and from group activity and we shall consider both these aspects. But once music ceases to give pleasure to young children then it ceases to be worth teaching, and this is a point that many teachers need to consider very carefully. To be a pleasure to the children, music must also be a pleasure to the teacher. When it is not, the reason may well be that the teacher is too conscious of its difficulties. These are real enough. But we hope to show that pleasure can be gained from much simpler activities than is generally realized, and we hope to encourage the diffident teacher as well as to suggest new ideas to the more experienced.

In some schools the teaching of music is still neatly divided into three categories: singing, theory, and appreciation. Such a division is artificial, and can be harmful. Appreciation should permeate singing and all music making, and theory should grow out of these activities. A song can be taught through the reading of the notes on the stave, and this may be called theory, but, if so, it is theory in practice. The singing of a song can lead to the making up of an accompaniment on percussion or other instruments, and this, too, is an activity that involves theory, but it does not isolate it. Singing, playing, moving, and listening should all be related to each other as far as is practicable, and the best kind of music lesson allows for them all.

Songs are the basis of the work suggested in these books, and ways of teaching them are dealt with later. They are not all arranged in order of difficulty as regards pitch and rhythm, but a suggested grading is given in Appendix 5. Although singing is the most easily accessible form of music making, it is not enough on its own to give children a full understanding of music and its possibilities. Music is sound, and at an early stage the exploration of sound will give an insight into its nature and into the various ways of organizing it to make satisfying patterns of pitch and rhythm. We have provided a number of opportunities for simple improvisation on instruments, and these lead to the playing of music from notation.

From time to time we suggest ways in which movement can be introduced. Movement is much more than a method of teaching children to listen. Music itself consists of movement from one sound to the next. Similarly the human body is constantly moving from one shape to another. In each case it is the way you progress from one sound or shape to the next that gives life and meaning to what you are doing. The character of the movement will vary according to the mood of the music. Sometimes it will be flowing, sometimes abrupt. Always there must be an inner impulse which gives logic to the progression. Not only can music suggest movement; movement can often help to suggest the rhythm and shape of music. If children are to use their bodies expressively, they must find out what their bodies are capable of. Suggestions for extending the range of their movement will be found in later chapters, but they should be supplemented by the books recommended in those chapters.

Listening is an essential part of music training. But bear in mind that listening to recorded music is not easy. When adults listen to records they bring a host of experiences to bear on what they hear, either consciously or unconsciously. For example, they may bring visual recollection of instruments and concert halls, or aural recollection of the music itself. These are only two among many ways that help the experienced listener to interpret what he hears on a record. But the child has usually had no visual experience to help him, and very little musical experience. He is thrown back entirely on the abstract qualities of what he hears, and it is not surprising if he quickly gets bored.

The child must first be trained to listen to the sounds going on around him, as well as those he himself is making. He must then learn to listen to his own sounds in conjunction with those made by other children; this is the beginning of ensemble playing, as also, for that matter, of group singing. He may then be ready to listen to music made entirely by others. The recorded examples suggested in the text all spring from activity which is itself the experience on which the child can base his listening. They are mostly short illustrative pieces that offer the imagination some scope, and they can all be found on the special tape that goes with Pupils' Books 1 and 2. There has been no attempt to present a programme of graded listening.

Although music needs no pictorial stimulus, it does have links with visual art. In some work cards we have used pictures as a stimulus to composition. The pictures in the Pupils' Books have a wider purpose. Sometimes they illustrate the text of the songs, sometimes they are extensions of ideas in the text and can be used for creative activity. But just as music is to be listened to for its own sake, so the pictures can be looked at in the same way. They provide a wide range of styles and colours; children will all find different things in both music and pictures and will often supply their own imaginative interpretation of what they hear and see. A word may sometimes be useful in drawing their attention to detail and if they wish to discuss the pictures, all the better.

The poems have a similar function and are generally linked with an idea found in the text or the music. Speech has a music of its own, comprising pitch and rhythm, and in this sense the poems are another means of experiencing these qualities. They can be read aloud by the teacher or by individual children, or they can be explored instrumentally or vocally. But they also have an intrinsic interest of their own, and it is for the teacher and the children to use them in whatever way they find most satisfactory.

Books and instruments are much more attractive when they look clean and neat. So equipment must always be in good order and carefully housed. But remember that children may well learn quite a lot when you are not there. They are great explorers, and, given the opportunity, they will sometimes teach themselves skills and even facts more quickly than they would learn them from you. For this reason they should be allowed opportunities of making music outside the normal timetable. If you lock the instruments away in a cupboard once the music activity is over, they may continue to look new and shiny, but you will deny your children the possibility of learning about music for themselves and enjoying your lessons the more. The dilemma can be resolved only if the children are taught to respect and care for the instruments themselves.

Needless to say, your own efforts are what matters most, and the better musician you are, the more confident you will be, and the more effective. Do not be too cautious. There will be times when you must be prepared to take risks. You need not despair if at first your efforts seem to fail; you can always start again.

2 Pitch and Rhythm

Most of the songs in the Pupils' Books have been chosen with pitch intervals and rhythm groups of varying degrees of difficulty in mind. The grading given in Appendix 5 suggests ways of ensuring a degree of continuity and progression in your reading scheme. But this does not mean that no other songs should be included in the singing class, nor that the songs in these books should always be sung in the order provided. They have been selected primarily for the pleasure they can give the children who sing them. We hope they will become part of the general repertoire, available whenever you or the pupils want them.

Just as children learn their early speech vocabulary by absorbing the language spoken around them, so they learn their musical vocabulary of pitch intervals and rhythm groups from what they hear sung and played to them. We suggest, then, that the early songs are taught to the children by ear before attention is drawn to their notation. The sounds must come before the symbols, and so elements of pitch and rhythm should not be isolated until the song is known.

Sol-fa

Sol-fa syllables are valuable for fixing pitch intervals in the children's minds, and in the songs in these books they are written above the notes of those intervals to which special attention is to be given.

Most readers of this book will already know the basic sol-fa syllables:

doh, ray, me, fah, soh, lah, te, (doh)

These are always in the same relation to each other and to *doh*:

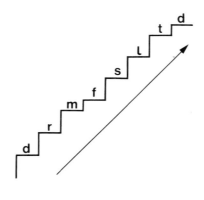

You will probably recognize them as they move up by step from low *doh* to the octave *doh* and back again, but you may not have met them in relation to leaps within this octave (e.g. *m–s*, *d–f*). It is important that you should practise singing these larger intervals to their sol-fa syllables as they appear in the songs, and be able to reproduce them accurately in order to help your pupils build up a systematic vocabulary of pitch. The acquisition and regular use of such a vocabulary is essential if reading is to become accurate and fluent.

Hand signs are valuable visual aids for impressing the intervals on the children's minds, especially since they show something of the character of each of the notes of the scale, as well as their pitch, in relation to *doh*. There is a diagram of them in Appendix 1.

The name *doh* is not permanently fixed to one specific note. Any note can become the *doh* of a scale. Try singing *doh* at several different pitches, and then build a sol-fa scale on each of the *doh*s you have sung. In these books a small square after the key-signature shows the exact pitch of *doh*, and from this the pitch of the other sol-fa syllables can easily be found.

If you can read staff notation you will be able to find the exact pitch of any *doh* used in these books on the piano or some other instrument, and this should ensure that the key of the song is neither too high nor too low for the children. If you cannot read staff notation, or have difficulty in doing so, you will find help in Chapter 3.

Time Names

Like pitch, rhythm should be experienced by children before they learn its technical terms or attempt to read it from notation. For instance, the following group is made up of two quavers and a crotchet, but such information gives young children no idea of what it actually feels or sounds like. If, however, they speak words in that rhythm, e.g. a name like Johnny Smith, or a sentence like 'Come with me', they will have experienced it for themselves, and after that its notation will be meaningful. In the early stages this association of rhythm groups with names, flowers, animals, football teams, and everyday objects is a valuable way of building on the children's own interests and rhythmic experiences.

But it has to be used with care. The rhythm of words can vary according to the person who speaks them, and the part of the country from which the speaker comes. We must make sure that we do not force words into a preconceived rhythmic pattern just to make a teaching point.

There is, however, a carefully graded and comprehensive system which provides an exact oral equivalent for any rhythmic group to be found in the songs of these books. Based on a method of teaching drum beats, it uses a pattern of syllables known as the French Time Names. These are all related to a basic unit which in Simple Time is normally the crotchet, and which is represented by the spoken syllable *taa*. The following table shows their relationship to this unit and to each other:

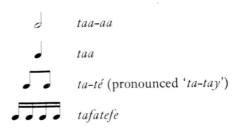

From these basic syllables other names can easily be worked out:

Teachers unfamiliar with the relative lengths of these notes should refer to Chapter 3; as also for definitions of Simple and Compound Time.

Time names are of value only as spoken sounds; their spelling is confusing, and they should not be written down as if they were words. They must be spoken so that their lengths are as accurate as possible; for instance in any song or piece of instrumental music *ta-té* must last for exactly the same time as *taa* in fact for one beat. Using these time names, the rhythm of 'Seasons' (p. 39) would sound like this:

ta-té taa | ta-té taa | ta-té taa | ta-té taa |

with each bar lasting for precisely two beats, that is, for two *taas*.

In Compound Time the beats are dotted crotchets, so 𝅘𝅥𝅭 becomes the unit of measurement for which *taa* is the equivalent. The basic time names are now:

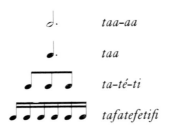

Other groupings can be worked out:

ta-é-ti

ta-tefetifi

Like the sol-fa syllables, the time names will be introduced to the children through the songs they are singing, and only after these have been learnt. Reading and writing will follow.

Sol-fa and time names are not ends in themselves; they are aids to the reading of staff notation, and when the children can read with understanding and accuracy they will no longer be needed.

3 Reading from Staff Notation

Not everyone who uses this book will be able to read staff notation. This need not prevent them from initiating many of the suggested activities, but it will limit their repertoire when they want to accompany songs on the piano, stimulate movement, join in instrumental ensembles, or pattern tunes—that is, play a phrase which the children immediately repeat in imitation. The process of learning to read staff notation on an instrument often sounds more complicated than it really is, and few of the tunes and accompaniments in this series will cause any difficulty to teachers who are prepared to spend a little time each day on practice. This chapter uses the keyboard to explain the symbols of staff notation.

Look at 'The Four Farmers' (p. 46). You will see two sets of horizontal lines drawn across the page and joined together on the left by a line and a bracket. Concentrate first on the upper set of lines as this is used for the melody of the song. The five lines are called a

stave, and at the beginning of them there is a sign called the treble clef: In this

book the treble clef is generally used for music played by the right hand on the keyboard or by a high-sounding instrument, or for music sung by children. This treble clef shows the letter-names of the notes which rest on the lines or in the spaces between them:

 spaces

The shape of the treble clef derives from an old way of writing the letter G, and so this is the name of the line round which it curls:

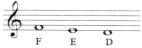

The space below G is called F, the line below F is E, and the note which fits under this lowest line is D:

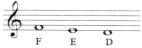

Be careful about the letter names *above* G. Only the first seven letters of the alphabet are used: A B C D E F G. This means that the note in the space above G is called A; the one on the line above that, B; in the space above, C; and so on.

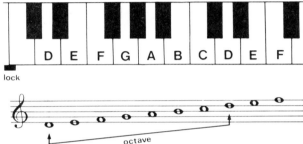

Now look for these notes on the keyboard. They are all near the middle, just to the right of the lock, and are played by the right hand. Perhaps the easiest to find is D, the white note between the pair of black notes. All the black notes are grouped in twos or threes, and the name of the note between each of the pairs is always D. Find all the Ds you can; they are at different pitches and an octave apart—every eighth note repeats the letter name:

Sometimes the notes of a tune extend beyond the five lines of the stave. When that happens, small lines have to be added above or below the stave to accommodate them; they are called *ledger* or *leger* lines:

Immediately after the treble clef there is usually another sign, the key signature. In 'The Four Farmers' it consists of a sharp placed on the highest line:

This sharp indicates that in what follows all the Fs must be 'sharpened', that is, raised in pitch so that you play not the white F but the black key to its right, as shown in the diagram below:

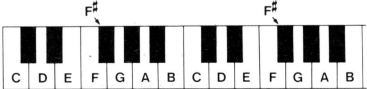

Some tunes have no key signature; you can play them on the white keys without using any of the black ones. Other tunes have key signatures which use a sign called a flat: ♭.

'We Wish you a Merry Christmas' (p. 60) has the following key signature:  This shows that all the Bs and Es have to be flattened, that is, lowered in pitch; instead of playing white keys for B and E, you play the black ones to the left of them. Chime bars and other melodic percussion instruments have separate bars for the sharps and flats, and these are clearly marked 'F sharp', 'B flat', etc.

Sometimes you will find a 'natural' sign in front of a note: ♮. This cancels the sharp or flat in the key signature (or sometimes a sharp or flat earlier in the same bar), and tells you to play the white note in the usual way. See for instance 'Rocking' (p. 56), bar 2.

As the word suggests, the key signature also shows the key of the melody; in other words, where *doh* can be found. All you need to remember is that the sharp furthest to the right is always *te*, and the flat furthest to the right is always *fah*. In what follows, *doh* is marked by a square:

Every piece of music has a fundamental pulse or beat that can be felt beneath the melody. Beats group themselves in 2s, 3s, or 4s, and at the end of each group a barline is drawn vertically down the stave. The music between each pair of these lines is called a bar.

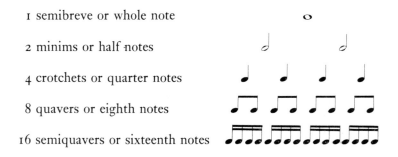

etc.

Bar lines

The figures after the key signature are called the time signature. They tell us how many beats each bar contains, and what sort of beats they are. The upper figure, in this case 2, shows the *number* of beats. (An exception to this will be mentioned later.) The lower figure indicates the relationship of each beat to the semibreve. The following table shows this relationship, and gives the names of the notes; it is meant as a quick summary for teachers, not for pupils:

1 semibreve or whole note	𝅝
2 minims or half notes	𝅗𝅥 𝅗𝅥
4 crotchets or quarter notes	♩ ♩ ♩ ♩
8 quavers or eighth notes	♫ ♫ ♫ ♫
16 semiquavers or sixteenth notes	𝅘𝅥𝅲𝅘𝅥𝅲𝅘𝅥𝅲𝅘𝅥𝅲

Thus $\frac{2}{4}$ means that there are 2 beats in each bar, and that these beats are crotchets or quarter notes. $\frac{2}{2}$ would also imply 2 beats in a bar, but this time each beat would be a minim or half note. The number of beats has nothing to do with the number of notes in the bar; the notes can be of any number and length that allows them to make up the given number of beats in each bar. In 'The Four Farmers' ($\frac{2}{4}$) the beats are divided like this:

You should now be able to read the complete melody of 'The Four Farmers' at the keyboard.

Now look at the lower stave. In keyboard music, including song accompaniments, this is normally played by the left hand. The bass clef at the beginning is a modified version

of the letter F– and this is the name of the note on the second line down around which

this clef curls. The other letter-names can easily be found in relation to this F:

You can now name the notes in the bass clef of the song, and find them on the piano, using your left hand. They are all to the left of the lock.

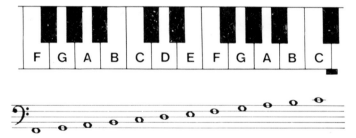

As well as symbols for sounds, there are symbols for silences. These are called rests, and they too are related in length to the semibreve.

	Note	Rest	Value
Semibreve	o	⬤	1
Minim	♩	▬	$\frac{1}{2}$
Crotchet	♩	¿	$\frac{1}{4}$
Quaver	♪	𝄿	$\frac{1}{8}$
Semiquaver	♪	𝄾	$\frac{1}{16}$

12

Earlier we promised to explain an exception to the usual meaning of time signature figures. The time signature $\frac{6}{8}$ implies that there are 6 quavers in each bar, but these quavers are not main beats. Each bar is divided into two main beats (♩.) each of which is subdivided into three smaller ones (♪♪♪). Look, for instance, at 'Billy Boy' (p. 99).

As you will see, each beat is worth a dotted crotchet, and a dot adds a half to the value of the note it follows. Whereas a crotchet is worth two quavers, a dotted crotchet is worth three. Thus both the notes and the beats in the above example add up to six quavers in each bar. When beats are subdivided into threes, the music is said to be in compound time; when they subdivide into twos or multiples of two, it is said to be in simple time.

Minims and quavers, as well as crotchets, can have dots after them, and this can happen in simple time as well as in compound. Can you recognize these tunes?

There is also a dotted minim in the next music example, but in this case the dot does not lengthen it enough, for the note lasts longer than the bar. It therefore has to be carried over into the following bar, and to show that it is merely sustained, and *not* sounded again, it is joined to its predecessor with a curved line called a tie:

The sweet notes of the night-in-gale flow

This particular note is held for three beats in one bar and for one beat in the next, making four in all. A tie always joins notes of the same pitch next door to each other. Rather confusingly, a similar sort of line is also used to denote slurring in recorder tunes, and in vocal music to show that more than one note is to be sung to the one syllable:

Go and tell Aunt Nan - cy

These lines are called slurs; you will notice that the notes they link are *not* of the same pitch.

4 Using the Piano

The Continuing Need for the Piano

Much classroom work can be done without a piano. But it would be wrong to neglect the resources provided by this instrument melodically, rhythmically, and harmonically. It is for this reason that we have included the piano in many of the activities in this book.

On Gaining Confidence as a Pianist

This section is not for those who have never touched a piano in their lives, nor is it for those who want to play Beethoven; such people should turn to a professional piano teacher rather than a book. But a book can help those who have just enough skill to pick out a recognizable tune on a keyboard, but not enough courage to do so in a classroom. The simple suggestions that follow are intended to break down your resistance to the piano. At first these depend on your ear rather than on finger technique or even the knowledge of notation; you may well be surprised at how much you can do with abilities you previously regarded as not good enough.

1. With one hand play by ear any tune you know well. Television or radio signature tunes are good for this purpose because you hear them so often. You will have to experiment to find out whereabouts on the keyboard to begin, but once you've discovered which opening note gives you least trouble you will have a small sense of achievement. Now play the same tune starting on one of the more 'difficult' notes; this means that you are playing it in a different key. Almost certainly you will have to use one or more black notes to make the tune sound right.

2. When you have worked out several tunes with the right hand (RH) alone, play the same tunes first with the left hand (LH) alone, and then with both hands at once. By experiment you will discover which are the best fingers to begin with. Such experiments may take a long time; don't be impatient!

3. Find the notes G A B D E, starting with the G above Middle C. These notes form what is called the Pentatonic Scale (which just means that the scale has five notes), and they are a useful and exciting basis for improvisation. Make up a tune with the RH using only these notes. Keep it short to begin with; as you develop a sense of what is good and

what is less good, you will be able to make up longer tunes. Now try making up tunes that fit simple poems; for instance, this one:

> The moon is full this winter night;
> The stars are clear though few;
> And every window glistens bright
> With leaves of frozen dew.
>
> Emily Brontë

Make up pentatonic tunes for other types of verse with, perhaps, six or eight lines. Listen carefully to the tunes as you play them. At first you will be satisfied with almost anything, but later you will become more critical. There are many qualities that go to make up a good tune; for instance a pleasing length to the phrases, an interesting shape, an arresting and easily-remembered rhythm. By listening more carefully to tunes on television or radio and comparing them with your own tunes, you will learn a great deal.

4. Instead of making up songs, try making up simple dance tunes. Your rhythms can sometimes be strong and exciting, and sometimes gentle and flowing.

5. So far you have played no more than a single melody line, sometimes with both hands at once but more usually with the RH alone. Now it is time for each hand to work independently. Find the note G anywhere on the keyboard, and play it at the same time as the D above it; the two notes are said to be a fifth apart (counting the bottom note as 'one'). Repeat this two-note chord in as many different rhythms as you can think of; first with one hand and then with the other; sometimes in three-time (triple) and sometimes in two-time (duple); sometimes with both hands at once.

6. Now repeat this chord in the LH, and at the same time play a pentatonic tune of your own invention with the RH, using the notes you've already learnt: G A B D E. You will find this difficult at first, but the trouble you take over it will be very rewarding. To begin with, make it a slow tune with a slow accompaniment underneath. As your skill increases, you will find you can put more energy into your playing. The music you produce will have a marked Scottish flavour, because bagpipes always play pentatonic tunes over drone accompaniments.

7. Eventually you will tire of the unvarying drone. The next step is to find other pairs of notes a fifth apart which can be used to vary your accompaniments. For instance F with the C above it will give your tunes a new and interesting flavour.

8. A pentatonic scale can start on any note. Try starting on C, D, and F. You will still be able to manage with only the white notes for the first and last of these, but when you start on D you will need one of the black notes. Which one is it?

All this work is likely to take several weeks, perhaps even months, but you will find as you go on that you are losing some at least of your fears about technical problems. What is vital is that you should learn to depend on your ear as the sole judge of what is good and bad, and your ear may well lead you to more varied and interesting experiments than can be discussed here.

Accompaniments

These ways of playing can now be applied to some of the songs in this book. 'Bobby Shaftoe' (p. 74) will sound well with a simple drone accompaniment. Such songs are so well-known that you will not need to 'read' the tunes from the book; you will be able to play them by ear. Next work out a simple drone accompaniment with the LH while you play the tune with the RH. Finally try playing the drone with both hands while you hum the tune; this is not as difficult as it sounds.

As you have probably discovered, not all tunes can be accompanied by a drone. Many tunes are based on the familiar major scale, and you will now need to discover how to build accompaniment figures on that scale.

1. A good effect can be made with a tiny handful of chords if they are carefully used. First you will have to become familiar with some simple chord patterns. For instance find the note G above Middle C, and then the B above that, and the D above that. Play all three notes at once with your thumb (1), middle finger (3), and little finger (5). This is a common chord of G major; such chords take their name from the lowest note. Now find as many chords of G major as you can up and down the keyboard. Practise building similar chords on other notes. Sometimes you will have to use black notes in order to keep the 'intervals' between one note and the next the same. For instance you will have to play a black note with your middle finger for common chords on D, on E, and on A; you will have to play two black notes for a common chord on B.

2. Now for the first inversion of the common chord. First, play once again the common chord of G major. Next, transfer the G at the bottom of the chord to the G above. This is still a chord of G because the notes have the same names, but they now come in a different order, and the result is called a first inversion because the chord has been inverted, with the G at the top instead of at the bottom.

3. There is also a second inversion of each common chord. The notes are still the same, but yet another of them has been transferred from the bottom to the top, so that, reading upwards, the notes are D G B.

A third inversion would be pointless, because you would once again have your chord in its root position. With the RH play these three versions of the G chord in differing orders until you can move freely from one to another. They form the basis of fanfares, so make them sound as though trumpets were playing.

Work out first and second inversions of chords in other keys, and ring the changes on them in the same way. Patience is essential.

4. You will not find it too difficult to turn your fanfares into a simple song accompaniment. While you play your three versions of the G chord with the RH, play at the same time the G below Middle C with the LH. (It usually sounds best to balance one note in the LH against three in the RH.) Repeat this process with chords in other keys; for instance C, D, F, and A.

5. Now comes a vital step; it will make your playing far more enjoyable once you have mastered it. Try mixing the chords you have worked out. For instance, move from G

chords to D chords and then back to G chords. Remember that when you change the RH chord you will need a new note for the LH.

6. It is now time to apply all this to a well-known song-tune; take the song 'The Spinning Song'. Play a common chord on G, and hum the tune in the key that chord suggests. You will find that G or D chords will fit all the way through. When you have worked out your accompaniment, turn to the setting of 'The Spinning Song' on page 42 of this book and you will find an accompaniment of the kind you have been aiming at. Elsewhere you will notice other songs based on the same simple chords, and if you study them you will be able to work out what to play for a great many other song tunes you happen to know and like.

Pedalling

Pianos have two pedals, and beginners should avoid them both. Nearly all teachers use the pedals far too much, more especially the so-called 'loud' pedal on the right. It does not in fact make the music louder; it should be called the sustaining pedal, because it sustains chords and notes, allowing you to take your hand off the keyboard without causing a break in the sound, and this is especially useful when it is awkward to get from one chord to another. This mis-named pedal is just as much of a help in soft music as in loud. Always take your foot off at the precise moment you put the next chord down, or you will have two chords sounding at the same time, and almost certainly the result will be an unpleasant clash of harmonies. In a classroom you are not likely to need the 'soft' pedal on the left. This is much more sensibly named, for by pressing it down you can soften the sound of the whole keyboard.

In pedalling, as in all else described in this chapter, the ear is the final judge of what is good and bad. More can be done with a critical ear than you imagine. Do not worry about not being able to read music fluently at first. When you want to begin reading music at the keyboard, refer back to the chapter on staff notation (p. 8) to check your knowledge.

Major and Minor

Not all the songs in this book are in major keys. Those in a minor key (for instance, the one on p. 90) cannot be harmonized without some adjustment of the chords described above. At this stage there is no need for you to be concerned with this, as it will be mentioned in later books.

5 Using the Guitar

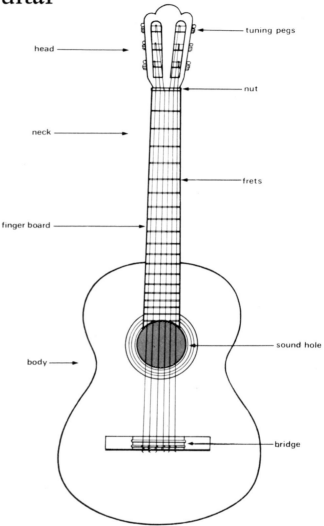

The guitar is a valuable instrument both for accompanying songs and for playing with the various classroom instruments. Many of the songs in this book need only three chords for their accompaniment, the chords known as I, IV, and V (see below), and these can be learnt by any beginner prepared to spend a little time each day practising their finger positions together with simple right-hand techniques. There are several types of guitar; the one described in this chapter is the Spanish or 'classical' guitar.

You will see that it has six strings stretched from the tuning pegs in the head over the finger board to the wooden bridge. They are numbered from right to left in the diagram, that is from high to low in pitch, and they are tuned as follows:

This is the actual pitch of the 'open' strings, but in any guitar music that uses staff notation the notes are always written an octave higher:

Before you start to play, make sure that the tuning of the strings is absolutely correct. This can be done with a set of six pitch pipes, but the more usual way is to tune just one of the strings, usually the highest (E), from a tuning fork or pitch pipe, and then to tune the other strings from each other. When your ear is satisfied with string no. 1, tune string no. 2 (B) by pressing it down just behind the 5th fret (this is known as 'stopping' the string), and it should then produce exactly the same note as string no. 1—E. If it doesn't, turn the tuning peg clockwise to raise the pitch, anti-clockwise to lower it. Next, stop string no. 3 behind the 4th fret, and it should then produce the same note as string no. 2 when played 'open'; again use the appropriate tuning peg if necessary. String no. 4 stopped behind the 5th fret should sound the same as no. 3 played 'open'; string no. 5 stopped behind the same fret should sound the same as no. 4 played 'open', and string no. 6 stopped in the same place should produce the same note as 'open' no. 5. If all the tuning has been accurate, the lowest and highest strings should sound exactly two octaves apart.

Now gently pluck each of the open strings from 6 to 1, striking them with the thumb of the right hand moving in the direction of the palm, and making sure that each string produces a clear, distinct sound. For this and other right hand techniques you will need to keep the finger nails a little longer than you may be used to—just beyond the finger tips; or if you wish you can use a plastic finger pick which can be bought in most instrument shops.

It will be clear to you that the six open strings on their own will not produce all the notes needed for song accompaniments. The extra ones are obtained by stopping the strings behind the frets in certain patterns indicated on the guitar tablature below, and for this all the fingers of the left hand are used—but not the thumb. The nails on these fingers have to be kept short so that the fleshy pads of the finger tips can press firmly onto the strings. The fingers are numbered from the index finger, 1, to the little finger, 4, and it is these numbers that appear on guitar tablature which shows pictorially the finger patterns for each chord. This tablature is easily understood if you compare it with the upper end of the guitar finger board in the picture on page 18.

G major

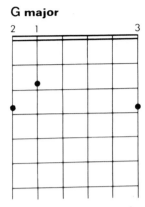

The double line at the top is the nut, the six vertical lines are the six strings, and the six horizontal lines the frets. The large dots represent the places just behind the frets where the fingers stop the strings, and the figures above show which fingers should be used. When there are no figures, the open strings are played; when there is a cross above the perpendicular line, that string is not needed in the chord.

Most players like to have a fairly high chair without arms on which they can sit well forward, and a small footstool to raise the left foot. Suitable folding stools can be obtained in most music shops. The correct playing position is shown below:

The waist of the guitar rests on the left thigh, with the whole body held firmly against the stomach and chest, and the finger board pointing outwards at an angle of about 45 degrees. It is very important that the instrument should not slip down onto the lap with its strings facing upwards. The right forearm should rest firmly on the larger curve of the guitar's body, leaving the right hand in position for the various finger techniques. With the instrument firmly gripped by the thigh and forearm the left hand is completely free to move up and down the finger board, ready to stop the strings; the thumb travels up and down the back of the finger board, roughly in the middle of it.

When you feel reasonably comfortable holding the guitar like this, find with your left hand the chord of G major as shown on p. 20. Hold this chord down, and strum across the strings from the lowest to the highest with your right thumb; if G major is the key, this is the tonic chord, known as I. In all keys the other two important chords besides the tonic are the subdominant (IV), and the dominant (V) to which the seventh note is usually added: V_7. Here is the tablature for the subdominant and dominant of G major:

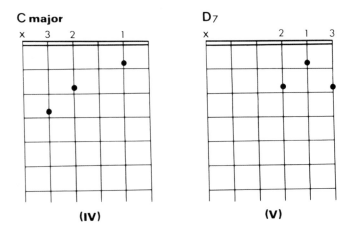

Some tunes in this book need only two of these chords for their accompaniment; for instance 'The Birds' Wedding' on page 110.

Others require all three; for instance 'Michael Finnigin' on page 76:

Get plenty of practice in moving from one chord to another while preserving a regular beat; count a beat for each chord that you play:

2 beats in each bar for tunes in $\frac{2}{4}$
3 beats for tunes in $\frac{3}{4}$
4 beats for tunes in $\frac{4}{4}$

For tunes in $\frac{6}{8}$ the counting will be the same as for tunes in $\frac{2}{4}$.

Here is the tablature for the basic chords in the other keys used most often in this book — C, D, and F:

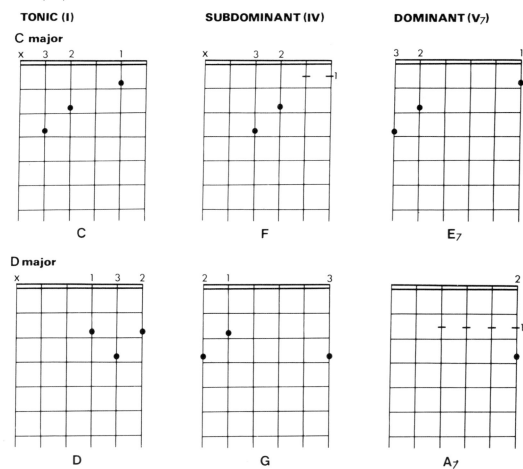

F major

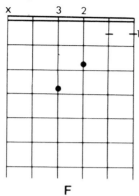

F

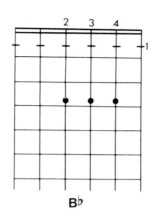

B♭

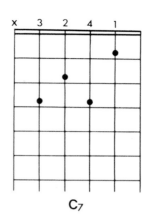

C₇

In this tablature a new sign is introduced; for the chords of F, A₇ and B flat the figure 1 is written at the side, with dashes on some of the perpendicular lines. This means that the first finger must be held firmly down in a horizontal position across all the strings marked with dashes; the player is then said to be using a 'barre'.

A useful piece of equipment for the beginner is the 'capo'. This is a movable clamp which, when tightened around the guitar's neck, stops (or frets) all six strings simultaneously. At each fret it changes the pitch of the string by a semitone; for instance if it is placed behind the first fret and the chord of G is played, the actual sound will be a chord of G sharp; if it is placed behind the second fret, the actual sound will be a chord of A. In this way it is possible to play an accompaniment at any pitch without having to learn all the chords of every key.

This cannot be more than a brief introduction to guitar playing. Nothing has been said about the right hand techniques, mainly because different writers use different terms to describe them, and those we chose might well be different from those the beginner would meet when pursuing the subject further. The following books will be found useful: *Hold Down a Chord* by John Pearse (BBC Publications) and *Introduction to the Guitar* by Hector Quine (OUP).

6 Teaching Songs

In spite of all the new and exciting forms of music-making that are becoming popular, we believe that singing will always be the corner-stone of children's musical experience. They can enjoy it at two quite different levels of achievement. A teacher who is proud of the way he teaches singing may give it all his attention and so produce one of those wonder choirs that fills the rest of us with admiration and envy. But not all music-making is intended for public performance. Singing can also be enjoyable at a much less formal level. Many songs do not need the polish which festival performances require, and they may well give more pleasure without it. How formally or informally a song should be treated depends on the song in question, and for this and other reasons teaching methods should vary from one song to another.

Strophic Songs

Many folk songs and ballads are strophic; that is, the melody is the same for several verses. A variation of this type is a song like 'The Trout' by Schubert, in which most verses are sung to the same tune but one or two have different music. With a strophic song, first give the children a general idea what it is about, and then sing the first verse while the children listen; sing two verses if the sense demands it. This is a vital moment, and you must summon up all your powers of expression to put the song across. Whenever possible sing from memory, so that you can look at the class while you sing. Next take the song section by section; this may mean line by line, but you will sometimes find that the end of a line makes an awkward stopping place, and that two together are more convenient. After you have sung the first section get the children to sing it back immediately without interrupting the rhythmic flow. If there are mistakes, do not stop to point them out, but repeat the line, still preserving the rhythm and emphasizing the right notes. If necessary, use your hands to indicate the rise and fall of the melody. Repeat the process for the second line. If this is secure, sing both lines together and get the children to repeat them after you. And so on. The whole process should be carried out within a steady rhythmic framework, and the response of the class should be alive—as it usually will be if your own performance has this quality.

Chorus Songs

Some songs have a chorus, always to the same words, at the end of each verse, and they can be learnt gradually by assimilation. After a quick word about the song, if that is necessary, sing the whole song, asking the class to join in the chorus when they know it. Alternatively, teach the chorus first. This, however, will seldom be necessary; it is good for the children sometimes to learn without realizing they are being taught, and you may well find at the end of your performance that they have picked up some of the verses as well as the chorus.

Cumulative Songs

Cumulative Songs (see pp. 88, 126, 150, 165 and 173) are also best taught by assimilation. As you sing the song through, the memory of the class begins to work, and by the end most of the children will be joining in.

Starting them off

Once a song is learnt it can be sung without your help, except that you will have to show the children how to start together and how to sing at the right tempo. If you accompany on the piano or the guitar there will be no great difficulty. Play a short introduction based either on the first two or four bars of the song or on the last two or four bars—whichever seems most suitable. (If you slow up your introduction just before the children are to come in, they will be confused and unsure of the tempo; play in strict time and they will know exactly when to start and how fast to sing.) But when a song is unaccompanied, or accompanied by the children themselves, you must be able to 'count them in' accurately. Most of the earlier songs in these books have two, three, or four beats. To indicate their speed, at least two counts are necessary.

> For a song in two beats, count 1 2
> For a song in three beats, count 2 3
> For a song in four beats, count 3 4

It is vital that you count at exactly the speed you want the song to go.

The above suggestions are for songs that begin on the first beat of the bar. But many songs begin on the last beat of the bar—with what is called an 'upbeat'. For such songs two counts will still be needed. For instance, if a song with four beats to the bar begins on the fourth beat, you will need to count '2 3'; if it has three beats and starts on the third, you must count '1 2'. Don't forget to show the children what note to begin on; either play it before you start counting, or sing your counting on the starting note.

Conducting

The kind of conducting technique required for a large choir or orchestra is quite out of place in the classroom, or even in front of a junior choir; those who want information about such technique should consult a book on the subject. In the classroom the primary need is to maintain a steady pulse which will keep the singers together; the time beating you will need for this purpose is not difficult to learn.

As a preliminary exercise, try beating time to a gramophone record, marking the pulses of the music with a springy flick of the hand. When this has become natural and enjoyable, start moving your hand in the conventional patterns; however many beats there are in the bar, the first is always a downward one and the last an upward one. Thus:

2 beats to the bar	A simple down—up pattern
3 beats to the bar	The first is down, the second to the right away from the body, and the third up
4 beats to the bar	The first is down, the second to the left, the third across to the right, and the fourth up

Two beats 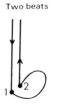   Three beats 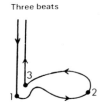   Four beats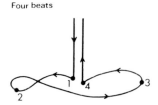

You will see that the hand seldom follows a straight line, and is constantly on the move from one beat to the next. Remember to give each beat a spring at the precise moment of its impact.

The above applies to music in Simple Time. In Compound Time the beats are sub-divided into threes:

It is usually best to beat only the main divisions of such bars; two beats for $\frac{6}{8}$, and three for $\frac{9}{8}$. But if the tempo is slow, you may find this uncomfortable and want to conduct each quaver, in which case your beats should follow this kind of pattern:

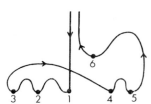

Professional conductors do not 'count in' their orchestras; they have a silent method of indicating what the tempo is to be—the preliminary beat. Classroom conductors can profitably practise this in front of a mirror. If a song begins on the first beat of the bar, give a preliminary upbeat on the fourth; if it begins on the third beat, the preliminary beat will be on the second; and so on. Always 'think' the tempo you want in advance, and make sure that this is indicated with absolute precision by the way your preliminary beat leads into the first sung beat. Under-emphasize the preliminary beat, and over-emphasize the one on which the children should begin.

In general, bear in mind that classroom conducting will not often be required of you; much can be done with facial expression and expressive hand movements. If you have to conduct for special occasions, try not to be self-conscious about it, and remember it is only a means of control and communication. Gestures that have no effect are not worth making, and they will distract your audience.

The following book will be found useful by those who wish to go further: *Conducting a Choir* by Imogen Holst (OUP).

Music Reading

The suggestions so far made about the teaching of songs imply that the children are being taught by rote, relying on their memory. Much singing needs to be done in this way, for our musical memories need plenty of exercise. But the process of learning can be speeded up by aiding the memory with the eye, and after a time, when children have learnt a song by rote, they can then be shown what the music looks like on the printed page. In this way they can begin to relate the musical symbols to the sounds with which they have become familiar. Some of the work card activities, and also some of the suggestions offered to the teacher, are designed to prepare the children for reading from notation. Instrumental work will give additional help in drawing their attention to the basic elements of pitch and rhythm.

What the teacher should know about pitch and rhythm is indicated in Chapter 2. Children will not at first be able to cope with both at once, and the two elements can to some extent be dealt with separately. Pitch is concerned with the rise and fall of a melodic line; to demonstrate this, sing one of the simplest songs indicating pitch levels with your hands. The very first song in Book I is stepwise almost all through, and many other songs have stepwise passages that can be used for this purpose. Ask the children to sing with you and at the same time imitate your hand movements. Then suggest that they follow the melody given in their books, with their fingers or with one end of a pencil. They can also try drawing the melody as a continuous line on paper or on the blackboard.

The next stage is the introduction of the sol-fa syllables; not all of them, but only those that are needed for a particular song. 'Seasons', the first song in Book I, is a good one to start with because it is based entirely on *doh*, *ray*, and *me*. Again the work should be done by imitation. Sing the song slowly enough for the children to follow and then let them sing from the printed page. Practice in stepwise melodies should be followed by the introduction of small leaps. Progress is bound to be slow, and too much should not be expected in the early stages.

All children have an innate rhythmic sense, but with some the pulse sense needs to be cultivated. At first give plenty of practice in clapping and playing on instruments the main beats in some song or instrumental piece. The children should also imitate rhythms clapped or played by the teacher, rhythms that the teacher keeps varying. They will then be ready to read rhythms from notation, though they will find this much more difficult. Begin with one of the earlier songs based on simple crotchet and quaver patterns. Sometimes the natural rhythm of the words to be sung can be used to demonstrate the musical rhythm. French time names will prove useful, though, as has been said earlier, they are not an end in themselves, and become less useful as soon as the rhythms implied by printed crotchets, quavers, etc., are understood. Appendix 5 contains both pitch and rhythm elements in a systematic order.

The amount of time that should be given to notation reading cannot be prescribed. A few minutes every lesson are much better than a whole lesson once a week. The pace cannot be forced, and teachers should be patient rather than risk killing the children's interest by over-insistence.

7 Classroom Instruments

Not so long ago the Percussion Band was considered an essential part of music in many schools. A sure sign of the forward-looking teacher was the box in the cupboard filled with triangles, tambourines, castanets, cymbals, and drums. Charts and scores were rolled up alongside the box and a whole scheme of rhythm training and listening was based on their use. Many children got a great deal of pleasure and knowledge from the Percussion Band, and, imaginatively used, it had great value. If it was not used imaginatively, that was not the fault of those who pioneered it, and many current ideas have a recognizable relationship with it.

The child is basically rhythmic, and if his melodic awareness can be developed alongside his rhythmic awareness he becomes more sensitive, both to the music he creates himself, and also to the music of others. His playing encourages his ability to make up tunes, and both activities encourage his listening. A major contribution has been made by the German composer Carl Orff, whose ideas have resulted in a fresh concept of the capabilities of young children. Many of the newer instruments now in common use have been created as a result of his work.

Pitched Instruments

THE GLOCKENSPIEL consists of metal bars over a long wooden resonating box. Each bar has its letter-name on it. In most makes the bars are detachable, and this enables the teacher to remove unwanted bars so that the child with just a few notes to play has only those bars in front of him. The basic set of bars is tuned to the scale of C major; sharps and flats can also be obtained, but only for those makes that have detachable bars. The glockenspiel is played with long-handled beaters, and these should normally be held lightly between the thumb and first finger at a suitable point of balance about a third of the way from the end. The beaters should rebound gently from the bars to allow them to resonate; this technique applies equally to the other barred instruments described below. There are two sizes of glockenspiel, soprano and alto; both are supplied in a wooden carrying-case that need not be removed when the instrument is played.

THE METALLOPHONE is similar to the glockenspiel, but larger and more resonant. Again, there are two sizes.

THE XYLOPHONE is like the glockenspiel except that the bars are made of wood, and it is not supplied with a case. A single resonating box carries the 'white' notes from C upwards; an attachment gives the 'black' notes as well. The beaters usually have felt heads, but as with other instruments of this type a wide range of tone qualities can be produced by varying the kind of beater. There are three sizes of xylophone, soprano, alto, and bass, the bass being the largest.

CHIME BARS are made on a different principle. Each note can be bought separately with its own beater and consists of a horizontal metal bar mounted on a resonating metal cylinder. It can be placed on any flat surface or held in the hand. A full chromatic range from Middle C upwards is obtainable.

Stringed instruments normally used in the classroom give a less percussive sound than those so far described. Some can be made by the children; information about their construction will be found in *Musical Instruments Made to be Played* by Ronald Roberts (Dryad Press). The two stringed instruments described next are easily obtainable commercially.

THE CHORDAL DULCIMER is an oblong box above which are stretched metal strings, generally in three groups of three strings each. Each group can be tuned to any major or minor common chord or 'triad', and triads on the tonic and on the fourth and fifth above or below it will provide enough harmonic accompaniment for many simple tunes. The strings are either plucked with the fingers or struck with a felt beater.

THE AUTOHARP can also be used for simple harmonic accompaniments. It consists of a small chromatic harp mounted horizontally on a resonating sound box, and it can be played on any flat surface or on the knees. Across the strings there are dampers labelled with chord symbols (C major, F major, etc.) and if you depress one of these dampers all the strings not wanted for that particular chord are automatically damped so that only the wanted strings sound when the hand is drawn across the instrument.

Two wind instruments are occasionally found in the classroom. THE MELODICA has keys, as on a piano keyboard, for altering the pitch, and its tone colour is such that it should be used with discretion. THE HARMONICA or Mouth Organ needs no description; the playing technique it requires is likely to restrict its use in the earlier stages of musical education.

Unpitched Instruments

THE CLAVES consist of a pair of cylindrical wooden sticks which give a sharp resonant sound when beaten against each other. One stick is held lightly in the left hand, lying across the upturned palm and supported by the thumb and fingers. The hand thus becomes a resonator, and when this stick is struck by the other (held in the right hand), the sound is richer than when they are struck together in mid-air.

THE CASTANETS most useful for children are made of two small wooden discs hinged together. These can be clicked in the palm of the hand, or alternatively they can be laid on foam rubber and tapped from above.

THE WOOD BLOCK is a specially-made resonating block of wood; it is struck by a wooden beater, and the sound can be very exciting. It varies in pitch according to the thickness of the wood.

THE TRIANGLE is the familiar orchestral instrument made of metal and struck by a metal beater. It must hang freely so that it can vibrate properly, but it will tend to revolve out of control unless it is suspended in the right way—on a piece of string or wire which passes through two holes bored in a metal or wooden bar as shown in the diagram:

The triangle will then hang facing the player.

THE TAMBOURINE is a small drum with metal discs or 'jingles' let into the rim. It is held in the left hand with the thumb through the thumb-hole in the rim and the skin facing the player, and it can be played by striking the skin lightly with the fingers of the right hand or with the flat of the hand. For a continuous sound it can be shaken with the left hand, or the jingles can be stroked with a circular movement of the right hand.

THE TAMBOUR is shaped like a tambourine but it has no jingles. Instead it has wing nuts in the rim with which the skin can be tightened to give a semi-pitched sound; the nuts should always be slackened when the instrument is not in use. The tambour can be tapped with the hand like a tambourine, but it is usually hit with a beater.

BONGOS consist of a pair of linked drums, one being larger and lower in pitch than the other; in some makes the pitch is adjustable. Bongos are hit with the palm of each hand or tapped with the fingers.

THE CYMBALS are usually played in pairs in an orchestra, but a surprising variety of effects can be produced from a single cymbal held in the left hand by a leather strap. It can be hit with a felt or wooden beater at any volume from very loud to very soft, and atmospheric effects can be obtained by drumming quietly on the rim with the nails or pads of the fingers.

All these pitched and unpitched instruments can produce a far richer range of sounds than the traditional percussion band. With their melodic and harmonic possibilities, they can now perform a complete musical score on their own, without the teacher having to join in on the piano, and equally they can provide a self-sufficient song accompaniment. Such accompaniments will be found later in this book, and it is hoped that teachers will themselves arrange other songs for their own instruments and players.

When building up a stock of classroom instruments, bear in mind the following points. Unpitched instruments are fairly easy to devise on the spot (tins, table tops, etc.), but pitched ones are not. It is therefore sensible to begin building up a stock of pitched instruments as soon as possible. The most flexible is a complete set of chime bars (C to G′ with all intermediate 'black' notes.) A glockenspiel and a xylophone, either soprano or alto, add variety of tone and should come next. Since work in groups is suggested in the book, the aim should be to provide five or six groups with two instruments apiece of varying range and tone quality. At some time, but not at first, a bass xylophone should be provided, since it adds a depth of tone sometimes felt to be lacking in chime bars and soprano or alto instruments. It also provides an essential starting point for bass clef reading, although this is not necessary in the early stages. Unpitched instruments are much cheaper to buy, and here again variety of sound should be aimed at. A wood block, a triangle, and a cymbal of good size and quality are suggested starting points. Hand drums are preferable to military-style drums. Drumstick technique is difficult to master, whereas it is comparatively easy to tap a drum with the hand or with a beater.

Always buy good quality instruments from reputable makers. Avoid toy instruments. Good instruments are expensive but essential. In many schools the financial allowance for music is inadequate, but it must be insisted that in this area of education as in any other, proper teaching can only be carried out with proper equipment.

Strings, Woodwind, and Brass

Not much can be usefully written here about the more sophisticated orchestral instruments, but it is an encouraging fact that in recent years they have been increasingly taught in primary schools. Today it is not uncommon to find children learning instruments of the string family, as also woodwind and brass, from visiting teachers, and some schools even have their own orchestra. A child who is learning such an instrument will be an asset to any class, and should be drawn into its activities as much as possible. The melodic instrument we have stressed in these books is the recorder, still a favourite in many schools, but it should be remembered that it needs as skilful and sensitive playing as any of its orchestral relations. If possible teachers should supplement the information given in Chapter 8 by taking lessons from a recorder specialist or by attending a recorder course. As some children will be more advanced than others on the recorder a few accompaniments contain notes not given in the first two Pupils' Books.

8 The Recorder

The recorder has become so closely associated with schools in recent years that there is a tendency to think of it as a modern invention designed to help children read music. This is a pity. In fact the recorder has a long ancestry and its own repertoire of beautiful music. It was particularly popular during the sixteenth and seventeenth centuries, in England as elsewhere in Europe. Henry VIII owned 76 recorders, and is said to have played the instrument with skill. Shakespeare mentions the recorder at length in *Hamlet* (Act III sc. ii) and more briefly in *A Midsummer Night's Dream* (Act V sc. i), and Pepys describes it as 'of all sounds in the world most pleasing'. 'The soft complaining flute', wrote Dryden, and like almost everyone who used the word in his day, he meant what we would call the recorder. It was used occasionally by both Bach and Handel, but by the time they died it had been superseded, at least in orchestras, by the transverse flute—the one that is still heard in orchestras today—and it was not until our own century that the recorder began to find favour again.

In its heyday the recorder was made in a variety of sizes, and it was played both as a solo instrument and in ensembles. When an ensemble consisted of nothing but recorders, it was known as a recorder consort. Less often recorders were combined with other instruments such as viols: the ensemble was then known as a broken consort. We hope that it will be increasingly used for ensemble work in our schools, instead of just for massed unison performances.

The normal recorder consort of today consists of instruments of four sizes and pitches:

The Descant (in C)
The Treble (in F): a fifth lower than the Descant
The Tenor (in C): an octave lower than the Descant
The Bass (in F): an octave lower than the Treble

The descant and tenor recorders, being in the same key, have the same fingering; similarly the fingering that produces an F on the treble recorder also produces an F (an octave lower) on the bass. The larger the instrument the bigger the stretches between the holes, and if consort music is attempted, the teacher will probably have to play the bass recorder because the children's finger-stretch is unlikely to be large enough. There is a considerable repertoire of consort music suitable for young children, by both early and modern composers.

As the descant recorder is much the cheapest of the four sizes to buy, and the most convenient for small hands, the remarks that follow refer mainly to that instrument. It is made in three sections, the head, middle, and foot joints, the last two being often in one piece.

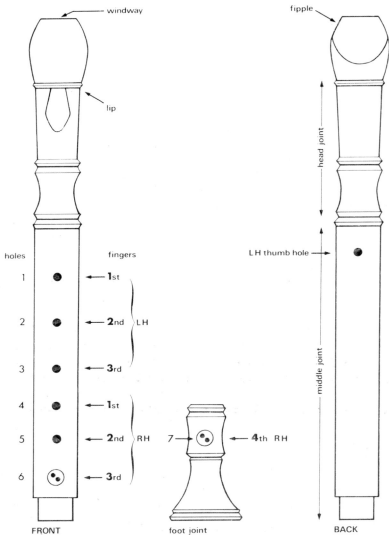

The sections can be unscrewed for cleaning, but should never be wrenched apart. Down the front of the recorder there are seven holes; the sixth and seventh are sometimes subdivided to produce semitones. In the back there is a single hole. The notes are produced by various combinations of fingers (or 'holds') covering the holes, and by the current of air directed from the mouth through the narrow 'windway' against the sharp edge called the 'lip'. Because of its effect on tone production this lip must be treated with great care.

For cleaning the head joint a feather is useful. Moisture in the air passage or near the lip can be removed by blowing sharply down the instrument while covering the lip with the forefinger. A piece of cloth pulled through the other two joints will clean them satisfactorily, but anything likely to leave fluff behind must be avoided. The need for cleaning will be lessened if the recorder is played with a minimum of moisture and, in the early stages, for quite short periods. In time the sections may come apart too easily because the waxed thread at the joints has grown worn and smooth. Scratching the thread with the finger nail may remedy this, and if it doesn't the joints should be rebound with more waxed thread ('lapping').

Whenever possible each child should have his own instrument. P.T.A.s and individual parents will usually help over this, once their interest has been aroused.

Now for the playing. Pick up the recorder with the right hand, and pass it into your left hand, with the thumb of that hand over the hole at the back and its first three fingers over holes 1, 2, and 3 down the middle joint. (In recorder playing we always speak of the thumb and four fingers, not of five fingers as in piano-playing.) The fleshy pads of the finger tips must fit well over the holes, with the little finger away from the instrument. When it feels comfortable in the hand, raise it and rest the windway on the lower lip, supporting the barrel on the underside with the right hand thumb—roughly behind holes 3 and 4. The fingers of the right hand will now fit easily over holes 4, 5, 6, and 7. The recorder should be held at an angle of about 45°.

Repeat this action, but this time when the recorder is balanced on the lower lip, remove all the fingers from the holes except the first two fingers and thumb of the left hand. Holes 1 and 2 and the thumb hole are now covered, and if you blow very quietly, just breathing into the instrument, you should produce the note A. If the note is sharp (a shade too high), use less breath; if flat (too low), increase your breath pressure a little. The pitch of any recorder note rises as you try to play louder, and for this reason players aim at a pleasing quality of tone rather than big contrasts of volume. In the classroom you can achieve such contrasts in unison performances by varying the number of instruments.

For the sake of clear articulation it is a good idea to make a quiet 't' sound before each note, and this is called 'tonguing'. When slurring is introduced (see p. 183) only the first note of the phrase should be tongued, that is, the first note under the slur. Suggested breathing places are indicated in these books by a tick: √

In recorder playing the fingers must move with precision, none of them leaving its hole until others are ready to take over the next position. When notes squeak, it is because one of the fingers is not completely covering its hole.

Always make it absolutely clear to the children when a note is to be blown, either by counting in or by hand movements. Some finger practice can be done without any blowing at all, the teacher quietly singing or playing the melody, but do not ask the children to finger without any sound being heard.

In the past the recorder has generally been associated with reading from notation, but there is much to be said for teaching by rote in the early stages—that is, by encouraging the children to imitate the teacher's pattern. Once they have a repertoire of four or five notes, they will enjoy trying to work out tunes they know that lie within the range of these notes, and they can also make up tunes of their own. All this will be good aural training, and it will help them to concentrate on the most important aspect of playing, the production of beautiful sounds. When they are familiar with the holds and can play a tune with a pleasing tone quality, they can then be introduced to the staff symbols.

We give below the basic fingerings for all the holds used in the recorder melodies in these books. Both the holds and the melodies are arranged in what seems to us a reasonable order of difficulty for learning purposes, but this order need not be followed if the teacher prefers another. The diagrams show the recorder as the player sees it looking down the barrel; the left-hand thumb hole is shown apart, to the left of the barrel. The diagrams are found in Pupils' Book 1, p. 64.

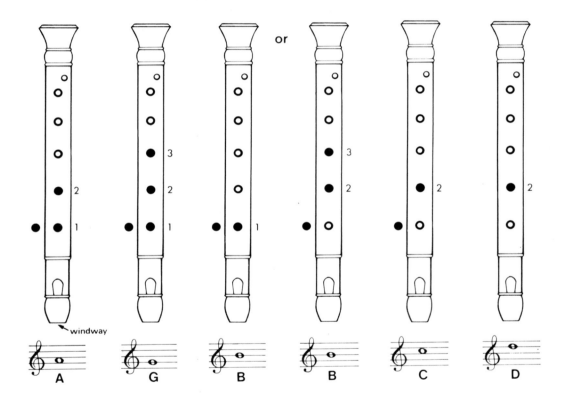

The first three recorder tunes in this book (pp. 40, 50 and 51) require only three different notes, nos. 4 to 6 (pp. 55, 87 and 106) only four. The others are based on the five-note scale from G up to D. The two pieces for two recorder groups (pp. 156 and 172) use the same five notes. All the tunes use only the fingers of the left hand.

In addition to these tunes, which are identified by a recorder symbol, you will find throughout the text further tunes which can be drawn on for a variety of purposes. Some can be used to illustrate points that have arisen in a lesson. Some may be suitable for reading either vocally or on instruments, if the class is advanced enough. Some can be arranged with simple accompaniments for classroom instruments, and some can be played on stringed instruments or recorders. You may also find that they are useful for movement. They are given in the Pupils' Books on the pages shown.

9 Music and Activities for the First Pupils' Book

We do not wish to limit teachers as to the amount of material they should try to cover each term, but they will almost certainly want some carols by December. In this chapter they will be found on pages 54 to 63, and divide very roughly the material many teachers might need in the first term from what they might need in the other two.

All through the chapter you will find suggestions for activities that will help the children understand what music is about. They are to be used as you think advisable, perhaps as starting points leading to better ideas of your own. Some of these activities will need spreading over a longer period than you may at first suspect. It will often be best to divide the children into small groups, but some tasks are for individual children.

The work cards that go with these books are especially suitable for this purpose. They are intended to give pleasure, while also having an educational aim. For instance cards 1 and 2 explore the quality of instrumental sound, cards 3 and 4 explore word rhythms, and cards 5 and 6 derive instrumental sounds from a picture. You should always check that every activity on the card has been carried out. In many cases the results can be demonstrated to the rest of the class. The cards are also progressive and should be used in the right order. It may be possible to allow a few children to go away with work cards while the rest of the class is engaged on a corporate activity.

You will find sol-fa syllables over most of the song tunes, but neither they nor the French time names should be introduced at first. As suggested in Chapter 6, the early songs should be taught by rote. When they are familiar, attention can be drawn to the sol-fa.

Seasons

Welsh Folk-Song: Suo Gân

Words by Michael Lane

1. Sum-mer's past, now at last Leaves must fall, gold - en brown.
2. All must wait. Soon or late Na - ture stirs, life re - news.

Trees are bare, clear the air, Win- ter's cold ends the year.
Buds are seen, fresh and green, Spring will then come a - gain.

It is a good practice to teach songs without piano accompaniment. Standing in front of the class and looking at them while you sing establishes a close contact which is not always possible when you sit at the piano. Whenever you can you should teach from memory.

(If you play the guitar you should be able to keep contact and play an accompaniment at the same time. But note that not all the songs are suitable for guitar accompaniment. You will find a list of those that can be accompanied with simple chords in Appendix 2.)

When the moment comes for the accompaniment to be added, how will you begin?

Not, we hope, by just thumping the first melody note on its own. The first line of the accompaniment might be effective as an introduction. As an alternative to the piano, melodic instruments can be used by the children as an accompaniment. If you have a bass xylophone, the LH part can be played as it stands; otherwise it must be played an octave higher, as indeed must the RH part which, as written, goes lower than most of your melodic instruments can manage. The parts are so simple that they can be taught by rote. Remember to remove all unwanted notes from xylophones and glockenspiels.

This little song suggests slow movement. As a movement activity, explore stillness and slowness with the children. Without using music, ask them to reach as high as they can, and then as low as they can. Now ask them to choose a high place in the air and move their hands towards it very slowly; then the same with a low place. Similarly they can move to high and low places with their elbows, shoulders, and head. They should do all these movements very steadily, finding various ways of reaching the finishing-point; not necessarily in a straight line. Move amongst them, and encourage good movement. If you feel the need for some accompanying sound, use a cymbal with a soft stick. Develop slow movement in other ways; from side to side, perhaps, or from one place on the floor to another.

As a contrast, sometimes work with quick movements. Always choose for accompaniment an instrument that seems to reflect the kind of movement you want. A cymbal might not be a good instrument for encouraging quick movement; could a wood block or tambour be better?

Chong Chong Nai

Pupils' Book p. 2

Malaysian Folk Tune

Who's Dat Yonder?

Pupils' Book p. 4

Negro Spiritual

Another three-note song. It needs to be sung with great vigour. Do not make a break between verses; keep strict time all through. The tricky rhythm in bar 4 need not be explained. It is far better to feel it than to try to read it from notation. The third note in this bar comes just before the second beat; both you and the children will understand this if you say the words as you clap the beats.

The Spinning Song

Norwegian Folk-Song

Translated by Anne Mendoza

Spin-ning wheel is turn - ing, Spin-ning, spin-ning, whirl - ing;

Pink and yel-low, white and blue, Co-lours of a {dress}{shirt} for you.

Not of silk and not of wool, But of flow-ers it is full.

Spin-ning wheel is turn - ing, Spin-ning, spin-ning, whirl - ing.

Teach from memory as far as possible, and try not to glance at the music. When you need the piano, the first two bars of the LH stave will make a good introduction. For variety, sometimes play the RH stave an octave higher.

'Seasons' used only three notes: *doh*, *ray*, and *me*. This song adds high and low *soh*. When the children have learnt the song, ask them which of its notes did not occur in 'Seasons'. The interval *doh-soh*₁ is an important one, and it occurs twice. Using the G and D chime bars, invent a jingle on some topical subject to fit these two notes, and teach it to the class; this will help to fix the interval in their minds.

The spinning wheel suggests a circular motion. Ask the children what other circles they can think of; the sun, the moon, a clock face, a circus ring. Ask them to move some part of their body in circles while standing still, starting with their arms. Let them make circles with a partner, sometimes separately and sometimes intertwined. A figure 8 is made up of two circles; suggest that the children make eights together; high above their heads and low down. They can also make circles with their feet—small ones, large ones, figure eights —singly and in pairs. Most singing games are circle games, and you will find information about them in *Singing Games for Recreation*, 5 books, by Janet Tobitt (A. & C. Black) or the two *Clarendon Books of Singing Games* by Herbert Wiseman and Sydney Northcote (OUP).

The movement ideas that have so far been suggested have grown out of the songs them-selves, 'Seasons' and 'The Spinning Song'. Many other songs in this book will suggest to you similar opportunities for movement, even when none is mentioned in the text. Two useful books on movement are *Music, Movement, and Mime* by Vera Gray and Rachel Percival (OUP) and *Movement in Sound and Silence* by V. R. Bruce (G. Bell).

The picture of circles (Pupils' Book p. 5) links with the song and the movement. It may also link with the first work card where part of the activity is to 'go from soft to loud and back again' in a kind of musical circle.

Khasi's Lullaby

Himalayan Folk-Song

Collected by Mary Rowland

Ha - ri cu - cu, ha - ri cu - cu,_ ha - ri cu - cu_ e - le.

Ha - ri cu - cu, ha - ri cu - cu, ha - ri cu - cu_ e - le. e - le.

As you sing this song to the children, show the rise and fall of the melody with your hands. When the children sing, encourage them to imitate your movements. Explain that the Himalayas are mountains; show pictures of Everest and other mountains. Ask one of the children to draw the rise and fall of the melody on the blackboard; the result will suggest a mountain range, and this simple act will draw attention to an important aspect of melody.

The accompaniment is written for piano, but it can be played on glockenspiels, and simplified if necessary; here are three possible patterns that can be repeated throughout the song:

The fourth degree of the scale is introduced in the melody of this song, and the sol-fa syllable is *fah*; also the sixth degree, *lah*.

Here is another way your children can respond to variations in pitch. Divide them into three groups. The first group should have instruments of high pitch, such as high chime bars, soprano glockenspiels, descant recorder tops. The second group should have instruments of low pitch, such as alto glockenspiels, alto and bass xylophones, and low chime bars. The third group should have unpitched instruments. Begin by asking the two groups of pitched instruments to make very quiet sounds in response to the high and low movements of your hands, each group responding only to the appropriate movement. The sounds can be sometimes short, sometimes long. (How does a xylophone make a long sound?) Your hand movements can indicate length as well as pitch. Now let the unpitched group join in. They will not be able to respond to pitch, but they can make sounds of differing length. Finally devise a very simple rhythmic pattern for the unpitched group to play while you indicate pitch patterns to the others. For instance:

This modest activity is a starting point for training in aural discrimination. It encourages the children to respond both to variations in pitch and to a regular pulse, and it encourages a sensitive use of the instruments.

There are several pictures of mothers and children in the Pupils' Books which can be compared. The one on p. 6 is Nepalese.

46

The Four Farmers

Roger Fiske

1. Far - mer Higgs, Far - mer Higgs, Far - mer Higgs has three black pigs,
2. Far - mer Howes, Far - mer Howes, Far - mer Howes has two brown cows,

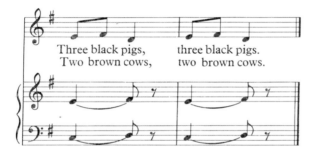

Three black pigs, three black pigs.
Two brown cows, two brown cows.

3. Farmer Penn, Farmer Penn,
   Farmer Penn has just one hen,
   Just one hen, just one hen.

4. Farmer Hall, Farmer Hall,
   Farmer Hall has nothing at all,
   Nothing at all, nothing at all.

As an introduction, play bar 1 of the accompaniment twice, at exactly the speed you wish to take the song.

'The Four Farmers' would be a good song to introduce French time names:

Ta-té taa | ta-té taa | ta-té ta-té | ta-té taa | etc.

Ask the children if they can think of an earlier song in this book which has the *ta-té taa* rhythm of bars 1 and 2. In fact the first five songs have been almost entirely based on the following rhythm patterns:

Write these on the blackboard as set out above. Pointing to each in turn, ask the children to play or clap. It will be best to work in units of four bars, so one of the patterns will always have to come twice. Keep the pulse constant as you move from one to another. Vary the order of the bars so that the children have to think more carefully. Finally turn to 'The Spinning Song'. Divide the class into halves, and ask each half to clap two bars alternately throughout the song. Any of these activities can be repeated with the children saying the French time names as they clap.

Here is a short traditional verse to say to the children. Do not try to make a musical point out of it; musical rhythms are not always the same as word rhythms.

A Charm to Cure Hiccups Pupils' Book p. 7

Hiccup, hiccup, go away,
Come again another day;
Hiccup, hiccup, when I bake,
I'll give you a butter-cake.

Traditional

Listen to 'Le Basque' by Marin Marais (no. 1 on the tape); its rhythm is similar to that in 'The Spinning Song' and in the 'Hiccup' verse.

Down by the Crystal Fountain

Pupils' Book p. 8

French Folk-Song

Translated by Michael Lane

Flowing but not fast

1. Down   by the crys-tal foun-tain, Sun   shi-ning through the tree;
2. Sing,   night-in-gale a-bove me, Sing   in the chest-nut tree.

Shines   on the crys-tal foun-tain, Bright   co-lours I can see.
Why   have you no bright co-lours? Hap - py you seem to be.

I think of you by the foun-tain, Do you ev-er think of me?

This song, like the 'Spinning Song', has a pitch range from low *soh* to high *soh*.

The first verse of this song offers a chance of developing ideas about water. Discuss the subject with the children, and choose one aspect of it; for instance a rainstorm. If you have room, seat the children in a semicircle, each with an instrument. Include recorders, and do not forget the piano. Pointing at the children, move your finger slowly round the semicircle; each child must play when your finger points at him. Experiment with varying degrees of loudness and length. Next try various groups with two or more children playing together. Don't always point in order; surprise the children. In one sense the sounds will be random, without any key, pitch, or rhythm, but this activity is not intended to produce organized music; its purpose is purely illustrative and imaginative. As the children play, the sounds they hear may suggest ways of illustrating a rainstorm. A storm has its own shape; it begins with a few drops of rain and perhaps a soft roll of distant thunder. The raindrops increase in number and speed until there is a downpour, with loud thunder and lightning flashes. Finally the storm dies away as it began. Discuss with the children which instruments will best express the different aspects of the storm, and try to ensure that they keep to what was decided in advance. The chief difference between a natural storm and a musical one is that the latter must be controlled to make its effect.

Listen with the children to the storm music in Rossini's overture *William Tell* (no. 2 on the tape) and notice the shape. It is the second of the overture's four sections and quite short.

The picture (Pupils' Book p. 9) is possibly more evocative than a conventional one of a storm, and may help the discussion that has been suggested.

50

Dance Tune

Pupils' Book p. 9

Hungarian Folk Tune

Pupils' Book p. 10

Collected by Béla Bartók

Fairly fast

Mister Rabbit

Pupils' Book p. 11

American Folk-Song

This is the first song in the book which uses all the notes of the pentatonic scale: *doh, ray, me, soh, lah.*

The accompaniment can be played on piano, guitar, or autoharp. If the autoharp is used, the last five bars of the accompaniment should be played as simple chords in the rhythm of the bass.

The first four bars may be sung very freely, making the rests longer if you wish. The last five must be sung in time. The song will be effective if you sing the first four bars of the first verse yourself, and the children respond with the last five. In the other verses they will want to be the rabbit and come in at bar 3.

Winter   Pupils' Book p. 11

Winter is here.
The air is cold,
The ponds freeze
As snow begins to fall;
Children play with their toboggans
In a white world.

Ten-year-old girl

Unto Us a Boy is Born

Pupils' Book p. 12

German Carol

first two bars as solfa ex.

1. Un - to us a boy is born! Lord of all cre - a - tion.
2. Cra - dled in a stall was he With sleep - y cows and ass - es;
3. Now may Ma - ry's son, who came So long a - go to love us,

Came he to a world for - lorn, The Lord of ev' - ry
But the ve - ry beasts could see That he all men sur -
Lead us all with hearts a - flame, Un - to the joys a -

na - - tion, The Lord of ev' - ry na - tion.
-pass - - es, That he all men sur - pass - es.
-bove____ us. Un - to the joys a - bove us.

If you say the words of the first two lines at a leisurely pace you will have some idea of the speed of this carol. Do not take it more slowly just because you happen to find the accompaniment difficult, but leave out notes if necessary; you do not need to play the tune at the top because it is already being sung. The bass is the most important part. The last two bars will make a suitable introduction, and the singing should then begin without any trace of a pause.

Ask the children to look at the first four notes: *doh, ray, me, fah*. Which of these did not occur in 'Mister Rabbit'? But it did occur in one of the earlier songs; which?

Dodo, L'Enfant Do

Pupils' Book p. 12

French Lullaby

Rocking

Czech Carol

1. Lit-tle Je-sus, sweetly sleep, do not stir; We will lend a coat of fur.
2. Ma-ry's lit-tle ba-by, sleep, sweet-ly sleep, Sleep in com-fort, slum-ber deep.

We will rock you, rock you, rock you. We will rock you, rock you, rock you.

See the fur to keep you warm, Snug-ly round your ti-ny form.
We will serve you all we can, Dar-ling, dar-ling lit-tle man.

The first bar introduces the 'doh chord': doh, me, soh. The carol goes at an easy pace, with two beats to the bar, not four. The accompaniment should be quiet and relaxed. Notice the LH minims, and compare the LH accompaniment of 'Who's Dat Yonder?'.

Encourage the children to invent their own Christmas lullaby, with a suitably rocking accompaniment. Give as many of them as possible two notes to play, either in the top half of the compass or in the bottom half; for instance:

TOP	BOTTOM
2 chime bars	2 chime bars
2 glockenspiel notes	2 glockenspiel notes
2 xylophone notes	2 xylophone notes

There will thus be one child at each end of the glockenspiels and xylophones; remove all unwanted notes, and make sure each child knows which of his notes is the higher. Subdivide these notes as follows:

TOP PLAYERS	{ Higher note	W
	{ Lower note	X
BOTTOM PLAYERS	{ Higher note	Y
	{ Lower note	Z

If all the children play their higher notes together, the result will be the note cluster WY; if they all play their lower notes, it will be XZ. (There is no need for these notes to 'fit' harmonically.) If the children play WY and XZ alternately, there will be some difference in pitch, but not very much; a more extreme difference is possible by alternating between WX and YZ, in which case each child plays both his notes at once. (You may not have enough beaters for this.) These alternations should be repeated several times with a steady beat—very quietly, to suggest the rocking of a cradle. Now try the four note–clusters on their own:

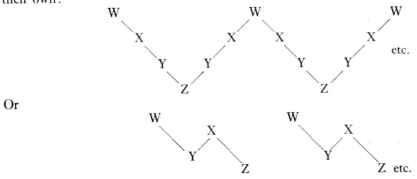

Or

This may remind you of bells. All these suggestions are very much easier to explain to a class than they are to express in print. The WXYZ symbols are for you, not the children. You can show them quite simply which cluster you want with high and low hand movements.

As soon as you get an accurate and quiet response, let the children who have no instruments speak the words of 'Rocking' over the playing. The speaking cannot be natural, and will be more like a chant, but do your best not to let it deteriorate into the 'Classroom Greeting' type of speech we all know so well. You may be able to find other and more suitable words for this activity; you or the children may like to make some up. Out of this chanting will come inflections of speech with risings and fallings. At a later stage these

58

can be turned into a more definite melodic line, but for the time being the mixture of these repeated patterns ('ostinati') and speaking will be sufficient.

The Baby King

Pupils' Book p. 14

Italian Carol

Translated by Mary Barham Johnson

1. Glad - ly the shep - herds Their sim - ple gifts are bring - ing.
2. Pro - phets and wise men In dis - tant lands are gaz - ing;
3. Here in a man - ger A ba - by small is sleep - ing,

Hark! do you hear them? Ho - san - na they are sing - ing.
Shines o'er the sta - ble A star with light a - maz - ing.
While earth and hea - ven Are in his might - y keep - ing.

O wor - ship him, O wor - ship him, Come, kneel in a - dor - a - tion!

D.C.—go back to the beginning (short for the Italian *da capo*—from the beginning); *fine*—the end of the tune (pronounced 'fee-nay')

Every year the shepherds come down from the hills around Rome and play their bag-pipes in the city squares at Christmas (Pupils' Book p. 15). This accompaniment is intended to suggest the drones of these instruments. The children can play the LH part on pitched percussion or the piano, and the RH notes on recorders (leaving out the grace notes). The carol should be taken rather slowly.

The whole of the melody can be used for reading purposes, but you will have to face the problem of the 'movable *doh*'. The first eight bars are in G major—with *doh* on G—but the next four bars are in D major—with *doh* on D. (You will notice that the key signature has not changed.) The children may already be aware that *doh* is movable, for it is on G in 'Seasons' and on F in 'Khasi's Lullaby'; they now meet two *dohs* in one piece.

Earlier we suggested that rhythm patterns from the songs should be put on the black-board for practice in reading. Now try the same activity with melodies. Write on the board in notation the first lines of four songs which the children have learnt; alongside write the words, but in a different order. By reading the melodic lines to sol-fa syllables, the children should be able to fit the words to the correct tune.

Venezuelan Carol
Pupils' Book p. 14

Translated by Vincent Morley and A. L. Lloyd

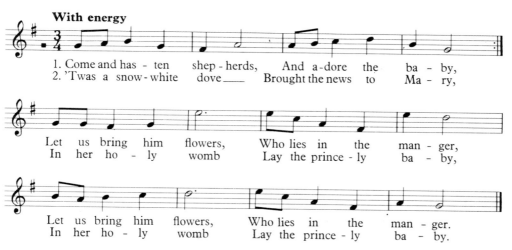

This is the first tune in triple time—with three beats in each bar. As always begin by teaching the melody to the whole class. It should be great fun, and sound like an energetic dance. But do not take the song too fast; the energy should come from well formed words rather than speed. It will sound best, not with a piano accompaniment, but with the following rhythmic patterns played by the children on unpitched instruments:

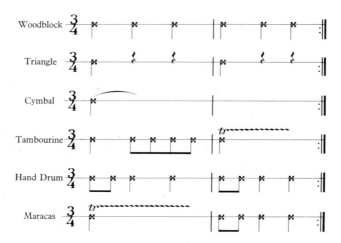

Children find it hard to maintain an ostinato pattern for long, so do not use all these patterns at once, but try them out in different combinations of rhythms and instruments. These are no more than suggestions; you may be able to find patterns which you prefer. When you have worked out your accompaniment, the carol should sound so strongly rhythmic that it suggests dancing. If it does, and if you have the space—then dance!

In this context the children may enjoy listening to two dances listed in Appendix 3: 'Son' by Leonard Salzedo (no. 3 on the tape) is in the Latin-American style, and 'Pandeirada' (no. 4) is based on a Spanish folk tune.

We Wish You a Merry Christmas

English Carol   Pupils' Book pp. 16 & 17

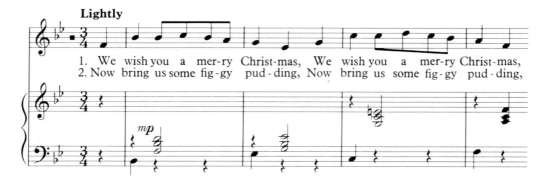

1. We wish you a mer-ry Christ-mas, We wish you a mer-ry Christ-mas,
2. Now bring us some fig-gy pud-ding, Now bring us some fig-gy pud-ding,

We wish you a mer-ry Christ-mas And a hap-py New Year.
Now bring us some fig-gy pud-ding, And bring some out here.

Good ti-dings we bring To you and your kin,

We wish you a mer-ry Christ-mas And a hap-py New Year.

3. For we all like figgy pudding, (*3 times*)
   So bring some out here.

4. And we won't go until we've got some, (*3 times*)
   So bring some out here.

This carol is sometimes sung too quickly; judge the speed by the clarity with which the children can sing the words in the quaver bars. The song needs vigorous performance, but it should not sound raucous or bumpy. Think of it as a waltz song.

As an introduction, play either the first bar of the piano part twice, or the last four bars of the melody in octaves. Either way there should be no trace of a gap between the end of your introduction and the start of the singing.

The Holy Child

French Carol

Translated by Sally Wright

Not too fast

Born on earth is the ho - ly child, Praise him with o - boes and bag-pipes play - ing;

Fine

Born on earth is the ho - ly child, Sing to wel-come the sa - viour mild.

(a few voices only)

1. For three thou-sand years and more Pro-phets have fore-told his com-ing,
2. O how trust-ing his smil-ing face, Safe in the care of his ten - der mo-ther,
3. Ho - ly Je - sus, the heav'nly Lord, Lies in the man-ger a ti - ny ba - by.

Cymbal (soft stick)

The first two bars of the tune are based on the '*doh* chord', but with low *soh* instead of high *soh*. The accompaniment can, if necessary, be played on the piano, but it is really intended for classroom instruments. Begin with the bass. The bass xylophone will be the most suitable instrument; an alto xylophone will sound quite well, but different. When this bass line is secure, add the voices. Next, add the tambourine, which should be played very lightly with the tips of the fingers. Finally, add the two melodic instruments, which can be chime bars, glockenspiels, or recorders; if there are too many notes for the children to manage, let them play only those marked 'x'. In the verses there should be just one instrument on the melodic line.

The early musicians in the Pupils' Book, pp. 20-21, are making music you can almost hear. What sounds do you think would come from their instruments? A new accompaniment based on these could be interesting.

To round off this short group of Christmas carols, it would be interesting to bring together some of your earlier experiments in sound. The pitch response exercise (p. 45), the storm (p. 49), and the lullaby (p. 57) might be used as they stand: they might also suggest other ways of using instruments to illustrate the theme of Christmas. Try to bring your ideas together in a sequence of words, songs, and instrumental music.

First you will need to decide with the children the order of the sequence. It might be as simple as the arrival of the shepherds at the stable, a lullaby, followed by the shepherds' departure. But in this short scene there are many possibilities.

Now shape the scene in more detail. Do the shepherds come by night? If so, the sequence could begin with a freely improvised night piece in the manner of the storm piece. What are the sounds of the night? What would the shepherds have heard? What instruments or voices could best make these sounds? Do they all begin at once, or do they build up gradually? As the shepherds approach, what do they play? 'The Baby King' suggests bagpipes. Try using the drone from this carol (G D) on a xylophone; ask a small group to compose a tune for the shepherds over this drone on the five notes of the pentatonic scale, G A B D E, played on chime bars. The central moment could be the lullaby already worked out in the experiment on p. 57. How would the sequence end? Draw from the children as much of the material as you can and only add your own suggestions where absolutely necessary.

*   *   *   *   *

Abiyoyo

Pupils' Book p. 22

Bantu Lullaby

Gently, but with a swing

This lullaby is effective with no accompaniment at all. It is very simple, and needs repeating over and over again without a break. Help the children to feel its gentle swinging rhythm, perhaps by using your hands. When it is known, you may feel that a little variety would add colour. Try a simple two-note vocal accompaniment. A small group of singers can hum D above Middle C on all odd-numbered bars, and the B below on all even-numbered bars; ignore the incomplete bar at the start. Continue this vocal ostinato throughout.

Pete Seeger tells how this lullaby traditionally comes at the end of an African bedtime story in which a dragon threatens the children. They are given a charm which helps them to sing the song, and it has such an effect on the dragon that he begins a slow dance; by the end of it he is so lulled that he is easily driven away.

Make this story the basis of a musical project. Begin by filling in some details with the children. The action takes place in the evening at bedtime. How many children are there in the story? Where do they live? In a town or in the country? What is the dragon like? What noises does he make? What does he sound like when he dances?

The children can now make a long colourful paper dragon, each of them contributing a section. Put it on the wall to remind you all of him. The music that will illustrate this story must have shape, as must all music, and the shape will come out of the story. It begins and ends quietly at night. In between there is a climax as the dragon comes in. The climax passes with the singing of the lullaby, and then peace returns. Think of all this in very simple terms. What events occur at night? What sounds are heard? How can they be illustrated on your instruments? The dragon music can be partly illustrative, partly conventional; try a dragon march with 'eastern' sounds such as cymbals, bells, and triangles woven into a rhythmic pattern of four beats to the bar. On one or more pitched instruments a simple pentatonic tune can be repeated over and over again above the rhythmic pattern; it might well derive from and fit a few words the children have made up about the dragon. The central section of the music will consist of the lullaby, 'Abiyoyo'. Finally return to the quiet night music heard at the beginning.

The piece called 'Petit Poucet' (Hop o' my Thumb) in Ravel's suite, *Mother Goose* (no. 5 on the tape), is about a little boy getting lost in the forest at night.

Good Night Pupils' Book p. 22

Here's a body—there's a bed!
There's a pillow—here's a head!
There's a curtain—here's a light!
There's a puff—and so good night!

Thomas Hood

Gaelic Lullaby Pupils' Book p. 23

The song, the poem, the Gaelic lullaby, and the picture of a Zulu mother and child (Pupils' Book p. 23) form a neat quartet. Small sequences or collections of this kind are interesting, and suggest a line of activity worth pursuing.

Down in Demerara   Pupils' Book pp. 24 & 25

English Student Song

1. There was a man who had a horse-e-lum, Had a horse-e-lum, had a horse-e-lum,
2. Now that poor horse, he fell a sick-e-lum, Fell a sick-e-lum, fell a sick-e-lum,

Was a man who had a horse-e-lum Down in De-me-ra-ra.
That poor horse, he fell a sick-e-lum Down in De-me-ra-ra.

And here we sits like birds in the wil-der-ness, Birds in the wil-der-ness, birds in the wilder-ness,

Here we sits like birds in the wil-der-ness, Down in De-me-ra-ra!

3. Now that poor man, he sent for a doctorum, *etc.*

4. Now that poor horse, he went and diedalum, *etc.*

5. And here we sits and flaps our wingsalum, *etc.*

As an introduction, play the last two bars of the tune in octaves, the singing starting immediately on the fourth beat. For fun, try the chorus like this:

After verse 1: sing it complete
After verse 2: omit 'wilderness'
After verse 3: omit 'in the wilderness'
After verse 4: omit 'birds in the wilderness'
After verse 5: omit 'we sits like birds in the wilderness'

Do not play in the gaps; complete silence is more effective and compels everyone to count.

Mrs. Button Pupils' Book p. 26

When Mrs. Button, of a morning,
   Comes creaking down the street,
You hear her old two black boots whisper
   'Poor feet—poor feet—poor feet!'

When Mrs. Button, every Monday,
   Sweeps the chapel neat,
All down the long hushed aisles they whisper
   'Poor feet—poor feet—poor feet!'

Mrs. Button, after dinner
   (It is her Sunday treat),
Sits down and takes her two black boots off
   And rests her two poor feet.

James Reeves

My Goose

Pupils' Book p. 26

English Round

Why does-n't my goose sing as well as thy goose,

When I paid for my goose twice as much as thine?

This is the first round in the book, and thus introduces part singing. It is a four-part round based on *doh, me, soh*. Teach it first as a unison song; watch out that the children (and you) tune the high note properly, without scraping just under it. When the children can sing the melody without your help, divide them into two groups with, if possible, a space between them. Show the second group exactly where they must start singing—at the beginning of bar 2. Tell both groups how many times they should sing the round; with only two parts twice will be enough. Beat time very clearly, with a good preliminary beat. At first the results may be poor. The two groups may shout each other down, or lose the tune altogether. Don't despair! Try it again, and ask for quiet singing, with each group concentrating on getting its own part rhythmical and in tune, and not listening to the others. When you think they are ready, try the round in four parts, but if the results are unsatisfactory do not press too hard. The tune is a slender one and will not take endless repetition; leave it for another time.

Go and Tell Aunt Nancy

Appalachian Folk-Song

1. Go and tell Aunt Nan - cy, Go and tell Aunt Nan - cy,
2. The one that she'd been sa - ving, The one that she'd been sa - ving, The

Go and tell Aunt Nan - cy The old grey goose is dead.
one that she'd been sa - ving To make her fea - ther bed.

3. She died last Friday
   Behind the old barn shed.

4. She left nine little goslings
   To scratch for their own bread.

This song was collected by Cecil Sharp in the Appalachian Mountains. We have provided a piano accompaniment, but as an alternative the simple note patterns of which it is made up can be given to classroom instruments and taught by rote. The chord symbols over the first beat of each bar can be used by the chordal dulcimer, autoharp, or guitar.

'Mrs Button' could easily be Aunt Nancy or the old woman who had a little pig. She might also be the owner of the feet in the picture of a dachshund on p. 51 in the second Pupils' Book.

The Little Pig

American Folk-Song

A - hoo,   hoo,   hoo.

Last time only

3. And that little pig, it died in bed, (*twice*)
   It died just because it couldn't get its bread.

4. And the old woman grieved and she sobbed and she cried, (*twice*)
   And then she laid right down and died.

5. And there they lay all on the shelf; (*twice*)
   If you want any more you must sing it yourself.

This is another song that Cecil Sharp found in the Appalachian Mountains. It is particularly good for practising clear articulation. Make sure that each syllable is properly sung, with all its consonants, but don't make so much of this that the song ceases to be fun. The accompaniment is not hard, and it is meant to be descriptive. The RH part is not suitable for the later verses; if you wish, you can play the LH part on its own but divided between the two hands.

The tune is pentatonic, and it can be sung without the piano as a five-part round; the starting points come on the third beat of the bar, and are indicated in the music by numbers. In case you would like to accompany the round with unpitched instruments, we give some patterns for ostinato playing:

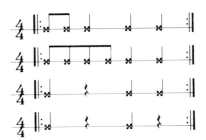

The following song was made up by a school teacher in the Appalachian Mountains. It should not go too fast, or be sung too loudly. A light percussion accompaniment will add interest. Ask the children which instrument they think will illustrate each verse best, and let it play only on the first beat of bars 9 and 11.

Sing, Said the Mother
Pupils' Book pp. 30 & 31

American Song

Quietly

s s s l s m m f s m m r

1. Ov - er in the mea - dow in the sand in the sun
2. Ov - er in the mea - dow where the tall grass___ grew

d r m m f m r d r m m r m d

Lived an old mo - ther tor - toise and her lit - tle tor - toise one.
Lived an old red___ fox___ and her lit - tle fox - es two.

'Dig', said the mo - ther; 'I dig', said the one;
'Run', said the mo - ther; 'We run', said the two;

And he dug and was glad in the sand in the sun.
So they ran and were glad where the tall grass___ grew.

3. Over in the meadow in a nest in the tree
   Lived an old mother robin and her little birdies three.
   'Sing', said the mother; 'We sing', said the three;
   So they sang and were glad in the nest in the tree.

4. Over in the meadow by a tall sycamore
   Lived an old mother chipmunk and her little chipmunks four.
   'Play', said the mother; 'We play', said the four;
   So they played and were glad by the tall sycamore.

5. Over in the meadow in a new little hive
   Lived an old mother queen bee and her honeybees five.
   'Hum', said the mother; 'We hum', said the five;
   So they hummed and were glad in their new little hive.

6. Over in the meadow in a dam built of sticks
   Lived an old mother beaver and her little beavers six.
   'Build', said the mother; 'We build', said the six;
   So they built and were glad in a dam built of sticks.

7. Over in the meadow in the green wet bogs
   Lived an old mother froggy and her seven little frogs.
   'Swim', said the mother; 'We swim', said the frogs;
   So they swam and were glad in the green wet bogs.

8. Over in the meadow as the day grew late
   Lived an old mother owl and her little owls eight.
   'Wink', said the mother; 'We wink', said the eight;
   So they winked and were glad as the day grew late.

9. Over in the meadow on a web on a pine
   Lived an old mother spider and her little spiders nine.
   'Spin', said the mother; 'We spin', said the nine;
   So they spun and were glad on a web on a pine.

10. Over in the meadow in a warm little den
    Lived an old mother rabbit and her little rabbits ten.
    'Hop', said the mother; 'We hop', said the ten;
    So they hopped and were glad in a warm little den.

You may like to make a round not from a tune but from illustrative sounds. Divide the class into three groups and choose three suitable subjects; for example:

Birds   A Farmyard   A Town Street

Talk about each in turn, inviting suggestions. Birds make sounds by singing, flapping their wings, rustling their feathers, pecking, hopping. Farm sounds are made by animals, machinery, running water, etc., and street sounds by walking feet, buses, cars, etc. The round will be like a journey which starts in the open country, passes through the farmyard, and ends up in the town. From each scene take just one sound which seems most suitable for illustration; use voices, hands, feet, but at this stage no instruments. Experiment with the children to find the most effective way of reproducing the sounds you have chosen together. Don't try to make these sounds fit into a time pattern. Feet tend to vary in pace when walking; people in a town stop to look at a shop window, and then run to catch up. Let the children make the sounds they think best, and encourage them to be individuals. Instead of conducting, allow about ten seconds for each sound, and then indicate the next one with a downward stroke of the hand.

Now try each group on its own. Group 1 will make feather sounds for ten seconds, change to machine sounds at your signal, and to feet sounds after another ten seconds. Groups 2 and 3 will do the same in turn. Finally treat the three groups as you would for a sung round, bringing each group in, one after the other, at ten-second intervals; the result will be a kind of collage in sound:

Group 1	Feathers	Machines	Feet	
Group 2		Feathers	Machines	Feet
Group 3			Feathers	Machines	Feet

Bobby Shaftoe   Pupils' Book pp. 32 & 33

Northumbrian Folk-Song

Fine

He'll come back and mar - ry me,___ Bon - nie Bob - by Shaf - toe.

1. Bob - by Shaf - toe's bright and fair, Comb-ing down his yel - low hair;
2. Bob - by Shaf - toe's tall and slim, Al-ways dressed so neat and trim;

D.C.

He's my ain for ev - er mair, Bon - ny Bob - by Shaf - toe.
Las - sies, they all keek at him, Bon - ny Bob - by Shaf - toe.

3. Bobby Shaftoe's getting a bairn
   For to dangle on his airm,
   On his arm and on his knee,
   Bonny Bobby Shaftoe.
   Bobby Shaftoe's been to sea,
   Silver buckles on his knee;
   He's come back and married me,
   Bonny Bobby Shaftoe.

Ain—own; evermair—evermore; keek—wink; bairn—baby; airm—arm

Notice that after the last verse the chorus words are different. Take this song at a good pace with the feeling of one beat to the bar. This means that the words must be clear and crisp, with plenty of mouth movement. The accompaniment is easier than it looks because the hands do not move about much. It can easily be adapted to classroom instruments, in which case you will probably have to take it more slowly. For this purpose put the chords into the treble clef and let one child play each of the three notes. As you will not be using the piano, try a rhythmic spoken introduction based on the words of the song. For instance:

The picture (Pupils' Book p. 32) is Rowlandson's 'Portsmouth Point'. Interesting sounds come out of this bustling scene. Can you do anything with them? A hornpipe for hands would be fun.

Michael Finnigin   Pupils' Book pp. 34 & 35

English Traditional Song

3. There was an old man called Michael Finnigin;
   He went fishing with a pinigin,
   Caught a fish and dropped it inigin,
   Poor old Michael Finnigin;
     Beginigin.

4. There was an old man called Michael Finnigin;
   Climbed a tree and barked his shinigin,
   Took off several yards of skinigin,
   Poor old Michael Finnigin;
     Beginigin.

5. There was an old man called Michael Finnigin;
   He grew fat and then grew thinigin;
   Then he died and had to beginigin,
   Poor old Michael Finnigin;
     Beginigin.

This is another word song like 'Bobby Shaftoe' and 'The Little Pig', and it needs to be sung with the utmost clarity. But it is also good fun, and it would be mistaken zeal to treat it like a classical masterpiece. Let the children enjoy it—but without shouting.

If you are confident enough, it is fun to raise the pitch one semitone every verse, and for this you will need to establish the new key with an extra chord in the last bar. We have included one example in brackets; if you are not going to change key, ignore this chord.

The accompaniment can be varied quite easily without altering the chords; instead, you can alter the rhythm. The following way of playing only on the last and first beats of the bar will promote energetic singing.

Heath Robinson's eccentric balloonist (Pupils' Book p. 35) shows the possible further adventures of Mr. Finnigin. Perhaps more verses suggest themselves to you.

Kumba Yah

Pupils' Book p. 37

West Indian Song

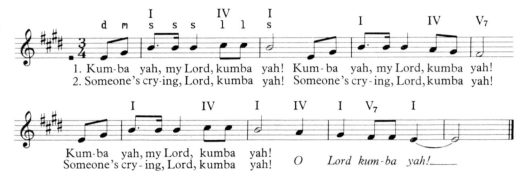

1. Kum-ba yah, my Lord, kumba yah! Kum-ba yah, my Lord, kumba yah!
2. Someone's cry-ing, Lord, kumba yah! Someone's cry-ing, Lord, kumba yah!

Kum-ba yah, my Lord, kumba yah!
Someone's cry-ing, Lord, kumba yah! O Lord kum-ba yah!

3. Someone's singing, Lord, Kumba yah! (*3 times*)

4. Someone's praying, Lord, Kumba yah! (*3 times*)

5. Someone's sleeping, Lord, Kumba yah! (*3 times*)

We have not printed a piano part. The character of this song is best preserved with a guitar accompaniment; only the simplest chords are needed. You might add a tambour, beaten very gently with a soft stick. The song probably derives from a Negro Spiritual: it has the mood of a lullaby.

The picture (Pupils' Book p. 36) is a very still one and seems to share the quality of expectancy in the song.

There's a Young Lad

Pupils' Book p. 38

Norwegian Folk-Song

Translated by Elizabeth Fiske

There's a young lad up the hill there; With his white coat and his bright hair

This song is short and could well be sung through twice. As an introduction, play the first two bars of the piano part; the singing begins on the third beat of bar 2. The bracketed notes in the middle and at the end can be played on instruments (using the higher notes) or hummed (using the lower ones).

Like the previous song, this one is in triple time, which can now be explained. Write on the blackboard four triple-time bars of crotchets and quavers on a single line. After you have indicated the speed by counting 1 2 3 (by way of introduction) the class should read them to their French time names, and then clap them. Now write underneath four bars in duple time for similar reading and clapping. By questioning, encourage the children to notice the difference between the two sets of notes. Now ask them to write two bars of notes in triple time or in duple time; pitch is a complication best avoided at this stage, and they need not put their notes on lines. Choose four of their attempts at triple time and write them consecutively on the blackboard; the result will be eight bars, which all should read to the time names and then clap. Do the same with their attempts at duple time bars.

Do not throw away the children's written notes; put them on the wall or in a book of tunes. They will seem more important to those who composed them than perhaps they do to you. At a later stage the children can usefully turn their notes into tunes, using *doh*, *me*, *soh* (on which this song is based).

Pant Corlan Yr Wyn Pupils' Book p. 39

Welsh Folk-Song

Turn the Glasses Over

Pupils' Book p. 40

American Singing Game

This song needs no accompaniment. Originally it was a singing game. Boy and girl pairs walk round in a circle with the girls on the outside; they hold each other's hands crossed, left hand to left hand, right hand to right hand. Surplus boys stand in the middle. At the words 'turn the glasses over' each pair raises arms and turns, so that the boys are now on the outside. They let go hands, the boys stand still, the girls go on walking in the circle. At the word 'lose' every boy tries to capture the nearest girl for his partner. Those with no partner go in the middle and the game starts again.

If you have no space for singing games or do not want to use the song in this way, try the words alone as a spoken round, bringing in each group at regular intervals, as follows:

Group 1: I've been to Harlem   I've been to Dover   I've travelled, *etc.*
Group 2:   I've been to Harlem   I've been to Dover, *etc.*
Group 3:   I've been to Harlem, *etc.*

Treated like this, with a different group coming in every bar, you will be able to have as many as sixteen groups, and the clash of syllables will make an intriguing sound. Alternatively try eight groups coming in every other bar, as marked over the music. Experiment with various dynamic levels from soft to loud, and try making crescendos and diminuendos —the children getting louder and softer in response to your hand movements.

Hungarian Folk-Song

Pupils' Book p. 41

This Old Man

English Traditional Song

Not very fast

1. This old man, he played one,
He played nick nack on my drum,
Nick nack pad-dy-whack, give a dog a bone;
This old man came rol-ling home.

2. This old man, he played two,
He played nick nack on my shoe,

3. This old man, he played three,
   He played nick nack on my tree.

4. This old man, he played four,
   He played nick nack on my door.

5. This old man, he played five,
   He played nick nack on my hive.

6. This old man, he played six,
   He played nick nack on my sticks.

7. This old man, he played seven,
   He played nick nack on my Devon.

8. This old man, he played eight,
   He played nick nack on my gate.

9. This old man, he played nine,
   He played nick nack on my line.

10. This old man, he played ten,
    He played nick nack on my hen.

84

An accompaniment on percussion instruments will provide a bit of fun as well as a little learning. You will need twelve players, and as many different unpitched instruments as you can muster. While the rest of the children sing, one child repeats the rhythm pattern for verse 1 throughout the verse; in verse 2 another child takes over the accompaniment with a different rhythm played on a different instrument; and so on. In each of the last two verses two children and two instruments will be needed. The quaver patterns in the last four verses may prove difficult at the speed this song requires; they are most easily played on bongos, with one hand on each drum. If you have no bongos, use two drums, or get the children to pat the tables or desks with alternate hands. All these patterns can be practised by the whole class before the singing begins.

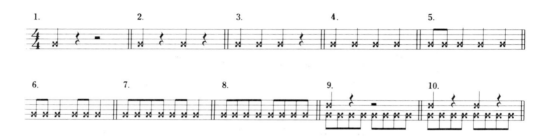

Later you can achieve a cumulative rhythm by adding each pattern to the one before until they are all going at once, though this is not easy. But it will show the children that rhythm patterns can be interesting on their own. Many primitive societies have thought rhythm more important than pitch, and jazz often gives pride of place to a solo drummer. At this point let the children hear a recording of 'Ritmos' by Leonard Salzedo (no. 6 on the tape).

A simple extension of the above rhythm accompaniment can now be explored. Give every child an instrument to beat; use all your unpitched percussion instruments and also a few chime bars and single notes on the glockenspiels, etc.; if necessary some children can tap their desks or any other surface you can think of that produces a tolerable sound. Now beat four fairly slow beats in each bar and ask everyone to play on the first beat only. When they can manage this, ask them to play only on the second beats; similarly with the third and fourth. In each case keep going for at least four bars. Always tell them whether you want the sounds to be long or short, and loud or soft, and vary the speed with each repetition.

Now divide the children into two groups. Ask one group to play on all the first beats, the other to play on all the third beats. As the children improve you may be able to try as many as four groups, each playing on a different beat. Listen to the sounds made by the different groups; notice that the sounds vary in quality according to the instrumental make-up of each group. By reducing the number of children in each group and by increasing the number of groups, a variety of sounds will emerge. These can be arranged in various ways to make a piece for one of Heath Robinson's machines.

The 'Cottage' poem has an obvious link with 'This Old Man'.

Cottage

Pupils' Book p. 42

When I live in a Cottage
I shall keep in my Cottage

Two different Dogs,
Three creamy Cows,
Four giddy Goats,
Five pewter Pots
Six silver Spoons
Seven busy Beehives
Eight ancient Appletrees
Nine red Rosebushes
Ten teeming Teapots
Eleven chirping Chickens
Twelve cosy Cats with their kittenish Kittens and
One blessed Baby in a Basket.

That's what I'll have when I live in my Cottage.

Eleanor Farjeon

Nine Red Horsemen

Pupils' Book p. 44

Mexican Folk-Song

Translated by Eleanor Farjeon

1. I___ saw nine red horse men Rid-ing o-ver the plain, And___ each held his char-ger By its long flow-ing mane. Ho
2. Their hair streamed be-hind them And their eyes were a-shine; They___ all rode as one man, Though I knew there were nine. Ho
3. Their spurs clanked and jin-gled, And their laugh-ter was gay, And___ in the red sun-set They all gal-loped a-way.

hil-lo, hil-lo, hil-lo ho! Ho hil-lo, hil-lo, hil-lo, ho! Ho

hil-lo, hil-lo, hil-lo ho! Ho hil-lo, hil-lo, hil-lo ho!

The chords under the voice part can be played on chime bars (with one child to each note), on an autoharp, or on a guitar. If you want to use a piano, you should work out some way of dividing the notes between your two hands, perhaps in a typical waltz rhythm; in this case use one note in the LH and three in the RH, as recommended on p. 16.

The scale passages in the refrain will be useful for reading purposes, especially those that do not begin on *doh*.

Windy Nights Pupils' Book p. 45

Whenever the moon and stars are set,
 Whenever the wind is high,
All night long in the dark and wet
 A man goes riding by.
Late in the night when the fires are out,
Why does he gallop and gallop about?

Whenever the trees are crying aloud,
 And ships are tossed at sea,
By, on the highway, low and loud,
 By, at the gallop, goes he;
By at the gallop he goes, and then
By he comes back at the gallop again.

R. L. Stevenson

In the Pupils' Book is found a trio of ideas—a song, a poem, and a picture. You could add an instrumental piece about hooves, harness, and wind.

If You Should Meet a Crocodile Pupils' Book p. 46

If you should meet a crocodile,
 Don't take a stick and poke him;
Ignore the welcome in his smile,
 Be careful not to stroke him.
For as he sleeps upon the Nile,
 He thinner gets and thinner;
And whene'er you meet a crocodile
 He's ready for his dinner.

Anon

Egyptian Folk Tune Pupils' Book p. 46

The connection between the poem and the Egyptian tune is slender, but the two might be used together. The tune has no speed marking, so that taken slowly it could evoke the sleeping crocodile, and faster could add interest to the more active beast in the illustration (Pupils' Book p. 46).

Bought Me a Cat

Pupils' Book p. 47

American Folk-Song

1. Bought me a cat, the cat pleased me,
2. Bought me a dog, the dog pleased me,

Fed my cat un-der yon-der tree,
Fed my dog un-der yon-der tree,

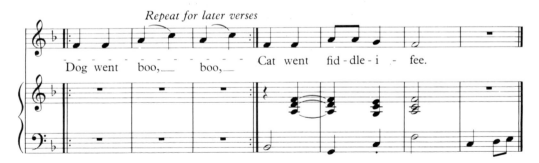

Repeat for later verses

Dog went boo,__ boo,__ Cat went fid-dle-i-fee.

3. Hen went ka, ka, *etc.*

4. Hog went krusi, krusi, *etc.*

5. Sheep went baa, baa, *etc.*

6. Cow went moo, moo, *etc.*

7. Bought me a calf, the calf pleased me;
   Fed my calf under yonder tree.
     Calf went ma, ma,
     Cow went moo, moo,
     Sheep went baa, baa,
     Hog went krusi, krusi,
     Hen went ka, ka,
     Dog went boo, boo,
     Cat went fiddle-i-fee.

A cumulative song. In the first verse the accompaniment is continuous, but in verse 2 three bars are left blank so that you can improvise sounds that suggest the dog. As the song goes on these 'blank' bars will increase in number and you will have to find more than one imitation to fill them. Ask the children what sounds they think would best suggest each animal. We offer two suggestions:

The imitations can be high or low on the keyboard, and include close clusters of notes without any harmonic implications, but if the singers get lost then you are being a little too inventive.

The Donkey's Burial

Pupils' Book p. 48

Spanish Folk-Song

Translated by John Horton

This lament should be sung softly. Pay special attention to the interval of a minor third (B natural—D) between bars 1 and 2; and of a major third (B natural—G) between bars 7 and 8. It is these intervals that give the tune its Spanish character. Notice the indecisive ending.

Because the song is in a minor key, you may find it impractical to use classroom instruments.

The Walnut Tree

Pupils' Book p. 50

Roger Fiske

With bounce

1. Bill Pal - mer the far - mer was not a clev - er man,
2. The wal - nut grew tall but it had - n't room to spread;

He plan - ted a wal - nut; that's how it all be - gan.
A big tree should not be too near a house, it's said.

He chose to put it close to the side of his house;
His wife Jill said — 'Look, Bill, the thing a - bout that tree,

It was - n't no big - ger than a - ny small mouse. mouse.
It blocks up the win - der so no - one can see.' see.'

3. To calm her, Bill Palmer said 'Never mind, my dear;
   I'll climb up and cut off the biggest branch what's there.'
   He had a long ladder, and with his large saw
   He climbed up and sat there; Jill stood by the door. (*twice*)

4. But while he was sawing, his wife said 'Look at you!
   You're sitting the wrong side of where you're sawing through.
   Oh Billy, you silly, you'll come such a bump.'
   As she spoke, the bough broke, and Bill fell down 'clump'. (*twice*)

The purpose of this song is to establish the intervals between *doh* and the other sol-fa steps that the children have encountered. The last line reverses the process and gives the intervals downwards from *soh*.

For the last verse the children may be able to suggest sawing sounds on their instruments, perhaps on the second and third beats of each bar. They will have no difficulty in providing something for the last word of all. The addition of a downward glissando on the xylophones will be effective; it should start at the top of the instrument on the word 'down' and reach the lowest note on the word 'clump'.

94

Leave Her, Johnny

Pupils' Book p. 51

Capstan Shanty

1. I thought I heard the skipper say,
2. The work was hard and the passage long,

Leave her, Johnny, leave her.

To-morrow you will get your pay.
The seas were high and the gales were strong,

It's time for us to leave her.

3. The food was bad and the wages low,
   Leave her, Johnny, leave her.
   But now ashore again we'll go,
   It's time for us to leave her.

4. The sails are furled and our work is done,
   Leave her, Johnny, leave her.
   But now on shore we'll have some fun.
   It's time for us to leave her.

Another pentatonic tune; it can easily be played on classroom instruments, and this will be a useful piece of aural work, but shanties, like singing games, are primarily for singing.

Tell the children a little about sailing ships in the olden days; shanties were work songs sung by the seamen to keep up their spirits and to give rhythm to such work as hauling up heavy sails. The capstan was used for pulling up the anchor; the men walked round, each pushing on one of the spokes, and a capstan shanty, with its strong insistent rhythm and marked accents, made the heavy work seem less arduous. These who did the work sang only the choruses. A shantyman, specially chosen for his voice, stood or sat at one side and sang the verses.

You can either have a small group of children for the verses and a large one for the chorus or appoint as shantyman one member of your class with a good strong voice and no inhibitions. Don't worry too much about the quality. Shanties aren't meant to sound as though they were being sung by a cathedral choir. Traditionally they were accompanied by a concertina or a fiddle, but they must often have been sung without any accompaniment; they can sound well without one in schools.

This and other shanties can be framed in a classroom composition about the sea on the lines of those suggested earlier about night and a rainstorm. Ask for ideas about the sea, its colour, its moods, and its sounds. (If you have used the work cards, some of the children will already have done some preliminary thinking on the subject.) Even if you decide to work in groups, it will be advisable first to do some instrumental work with the whole class. To stimulate their imaginations, invite suggestions for loud splashing sounds, quiet lapping sounds, etc. Some may be more realistic if the children use their voices rather than their instruments. Be clear in your own mind that this will be a purely illustrative piece of work, without any organized pitch or rhythm. Even so, there must be some kind of form to make the results coherent. It may be no more than a gradual build-up of sound to a particular point, or it may be a series of small events with those at the start returning near the end. This element of form is vital to the children's understanding of the way in which music is conceived.

When your sea piece has been planned and practised, it will be time for you and the class to listen critically. Does it really do what it set out to do? Could it have been better done another way? If improvements are thought necessary, make them, and then think how to link the piece with the shanties you have learnt. Will you sing first and then have the sea piece, or will the singing come in the middle? Would it be a good idea to sing the shanty at the same time as the sea sounds are being made?

Donald, O Donald

Pupils' Book pp. 52 & 53

Hebridean Folk-Song

Translated by Margaret Shaw-Campbell

Dancing

Don - ald, O Don - ald, To the moor the we-ther's gone,

Fine

Don - ald, O Don - ald, And the te - ther with him.

Hin, han, hur - ry O, I - sa - bel and 'Liz - a - beth,

D.C. al Fine

Hin, han, __ hur - ry O, Mc-Ca-lum's girl and Don - ald.

In the north-west of Scotland, where Gaelic is spoken rather than English, school children may prefer to sing this song to its proper Gaelic words:

Dhomhnuill, a Dhomhnuill,
Thug am molt am monadh air!
Dhomhnuill, a Dhomhnuill,
Theich é leis an ropàn!

(twice)

Hinn, hainn hurra bhi!
Isebeil is Ealasaid;
Hinn, hainn hurra bhi!
Ni' Chaluim is Dhomhnuill.

Dhomhnuill, a Dhomhnuill, *etc.*

Explain that the ram has pulled up the post to which he was tethered. The song should go with a swing and a driving pulse and rather quickly, and that is how you should first sing it to the children. The pace will be determined by the words in bars 2 and 4, which must be clearly articulated. In bar 6 the tune has an unusual twist, which you should first practise yourself. Note 1 in bar 8 is a grace note; it should be lightly touched just before the first beat. The accompaniment is written for piano, RH only; alternatively it could be played by a xylophone, but if so, it must not drag. The song can also be sung unaccompanied except for a drum beat, either on the first and third beats of each bar, or following the rhythm of the piano part.

If you manage to find the right pace and rhythmic excitement, the children's feet may begin to tap. If so, devise some simple steps for them as they stand in a circle. For instance:

Bar 1: RF (right foot) to the side, LF join, RF to the side
Bar 2: LF to the side, RF join, LF to the side
Bars 3 and 4: As above
Bar 5: RF forward, LF join
Bar 6: LF back, RF join
Bars 7 and 8: as for bars 5 and 6
Repeat steps for bars 1–4

The song can be happily sung as a two-part round, with the second voice starting in bar 2. At the same time it can be danced as a round with the children in two concentric circles; leave enough room for their forward and backward movements.

98

Birthday Round

Pupils' Book p. 54

Moritz Hauptmann

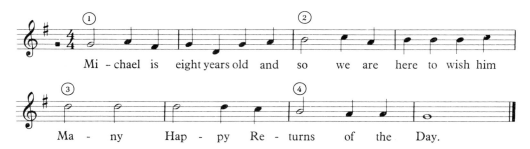

Mi - chael is eight years old and so we are here to wish him

Ma - ny Hap - py Re - turns of the Day.

The music of this four-part round was written by a nineteenth-century German composer named Hauptmann; he expected the name in bar 1 and the age in bar 2 to be adjusted to suit those who were singing.

It is not necessary in rounds for each voice to sing the tune the same number of times and then stop; it is at least as effective to make everyone stop at some given point, regardless of the sense, so that the round ends on a pleasant finishing chord instead of trailing off into nothing. Beat two beats to the bar, allow the fourth voice to sing the tune through at least twice, and then in any odd-numbered bar make them all slow down and stop on the first beat of the following bar; keep your hand in the air to show you wish the note to be held on. Make sure the children are looking at you and following your directions. At the first attempt there will probably be confusion, with some of the children going on singing after you want them to stop, but they will soon get the point, and enjoy the new sound of a three-part chord at the end.

Pancakes

Pupils' Book p. 54

Someone's making pancakes,
  The girdle's on the grate;
The bowl of batter's beaten up,
  So I am going to wait
Until the work is over
  And there, perhaps, will be,
Among the brown and speckled ones,
  A yellow one for me.

Elizabeth Fleming

Billy Boy

Pupils' Book p. 55

Capstan Shanty

Fast

1. Where hev ye been äal the day, Bil - ly Boy, Bil - ly Boy?
2. Is she fit to be your wife, Bil - ly Boy, Bil - ly Boy?

Where hev ye been äal the day, me Bil - ly Boy?
Is she fit to be your wife, me Bil - ly Boy?

I've been walk - ing äal the day with me char - min' Nan - cy Grey,
She's as fit to be my wife as the fork is to the knife,

And me Nan - cy kit - tled me fan - cy, Oh me char-min' Bil - ly Boy.

3. Can she cook a bit o' steak,
Billy Boy, Billy Boy?
Can she cook a bit o' steak,
Me Billy Boy?
She can cook a bit o' steak,
Aye, and myek a gairdle cake,
And me Nancy kittled me fancy,
Oh me charmin' Billy Boy!

myek a gairdle cake—make a girdle cake

The accompaniment suggests a fiddle, and it must be played lightly but with much verve. If you play the violin, why not use it here instead of a piano?

This shanty comes from Northumberland. Do you or the children know any other songs about Billy Boy?

The Swapping Song

Pupils' Book pp. 53 & 54

American Folk-Song

3. The lanes were so long and the streets were so narrow,
   I had to bring her home in an old wheelbarrow.

4. The wheelbarrow broke and my wife got a fall;
   Down came wheelbarrow, little wife and all.

5. Swapped my wheelbarrow and got me a horse,
   Then I rode from cross to cross.

6. Swapped my horse and got me a mare,
   Then I rode from fair to fair.

7. Swapped my mare and got me a mule,
   Then I rode like a doggone fool.

8. Swapped my mule and got me a cow;
   In that trade I learnt just how.

9. Swapped my cow and got me a calf;
   In that trade I lost just half.

10. Swapped my calf and got me a sheep,
    Then I rode myself to sleep.

11. Swapped my sheep and got me a hen;
    O what a pretty thing I had then!

12. Swapped my hen and got me a rat,
    Put it on the haystack away from the cat.

13. Swapped my rat and got me a mole;
    Doggone thing ran straight to its hole!

This song is a fine example of the continuing vitality of the pentatonic scale. You may feel that thirteen verses are too many, but if the pace is right the song won't seem too long. Some of the words need looking at before you begin or the children will find them hard to fit to the tune.

Pavane

Pupils' Book p. 57

Old French Dance

Peter Warlock's *Capriol Suite* is based on old French dance tunes, and includes an arrangement of this one.

Pirulito

Pupils' Book p. 58

Brazilian Clapping Song

Translated by L.J.

The rhythm of the first complete bar is a new and exciting one; it gives great impulse to the simple melody. The accompaniment should consist of clapping alone. Here are some rhythms to use as ostinato patterns:

You might sing the song three times with a different clapping rhythm for each verse.

Clapping can produce an extraordinary variety of sound effects. You can clap with

> flat hands
> cupped hands
> the tips of two fingers on the other palm
> the tips of four fingers

Each of these effects can be varied in another way; they can be done

> loudly
> softly
> getting gradually louder (crescendo)
> getting gradually softer (diminuendo)

Quite different effects can be produced by

> rubbing the palms together
> knocking the knuckles together
> snapping the fingers

In addition your hands can produce yet another range of sounds, with quite different resonances, by hitting flat surfaces such as a table, or the sides of a chair.

All these hand effects can be built up into a composition that uses rhythms but no tunes or harmonies. Work in two-bar phrases, using quite simple rhythm patterns; interest and excitement will come from precision and energy rather than from complicated patterns. Because rhythms without melodies are hard to remember, write down your patterns on the blackboard and teach them one at a time, then two at a time, and so on.

Invite the children to suggest what style of clapping should be used for each pattern, and when to have more than one style at the same time. You will have to be patient in helping the children to memorize the patterns, but when they have done so the result will be very stimulating.

The dancers in the picture (Pupils' Book p. 59) are Brazilian, and might well be dancing this song.

Spanish Dance Tune

Pupils' Book p. 58

The Greater Cats

Pupils' Book p. 59

The greater cats with golden eyes
Stare out between the bars.
Deserts are there, and different skies,
And night with different stars.

V. Sackville-West

The Girl Who Liked Dancing Pupils' Book p. 61

Swedish Folk-Song

Translated by Elizabeth Fiske

1. There once was a girl who liked to go danc-ing all day;
2. He said 'I am tied so tight-ly, my hand is quite sore;

She wished to be sure her part-ner would not slip a-way.
I beg you to loose the band just a lit-tle bit more.'

She came to the dance with a red gol-den band,
She loos-ened the band till the knot was quite slack;

And firm-ly she tied it a-round a man's hand.
Then he ran a-way, and he nev-er came back.

A song about dancing should have the feel of a dance. Much depends on your presentation of it; energetic rhythms, an expressive face, and a generally dramatic approach will get the sort of response you want.

The Cobbler's Jig

English Folk Tune

Pupils' Book p. 61

from Playford's 'English Dancing Master'

The Mocking Bird

Pupils' Book p. 62

Appalachian Folk-Song

Chime
Bars

Xylophone

1. Hush up, ba - by, don't say a word,
2. If it can't whis-tle, and it can't sing,

Pa-pa's gon-na buy you a mock - ing bird.
Pa-pa's gon-na buy you a di - a-mond ring.

(last time)

3. If that diamond ring turns to brass,
   Papa's gonna buy you a looking-glass.

4. If that looking-glass gets broke,
   Papa's gonna buy you a Billy-goat.

5. If that Billy-goat runs away,
   Papa's gonna buy you another today.

This gentle little song from the Appalachian Mountains needs a correspondingly gentle accompaniment. The piano might do as a last resort but it is really too robust, and the suggested classroom instruments will be more effective.

The teaching of instrumental parts always presents a problem of organization. What will the rest of the class do while they are being learnt? Here is a possible solution. Each of the three instrumental parts is a simple repeated phrase of only two or three notes, and as they all lie within the children's vocal range they can be sung to 'lah'. Begin by teaching the instrumental parts of the first four bars as a three-part round, starting with the minims in the top line. After four bars bring in your second group while the first switches to the lower notes in the top stave of the accompaniment. And so on. Each group will sing each rhythmic pattern four times. You can have yet another group singing the melody and words of the song if you think this can be managed.

When the sung parts are secure, ask one child from each group to play an instrument instead of singing. Finally ask all the children except the three instrumentalists to sing the melody and words of the song. Later you might substitute for the xylophone crotchets the same pattern in quavers:

Alternatively the quavers could be played by glockenspiels while the xylophones stick to their crotchets. Any beginners you may have on the violin or cello would also find these patterns within their powers. The music on the tape (no. 7) from Carl Orff's 'Music for Children' is played on classroom instruments with a cello. It consists of simple ostinato patterns in the same manner as our arrangement of 'The Mocking Bird'.

The picture of the peacock dish (Pupils' Book p. 63) is so fine that we felt it should be included. This peacock is far more beautiful than a real mocking bird, and this dish suggests a story like 'The Ugly Duckling'.

Post-horn Signal

Pupils' Book p. 64

Austrian Round

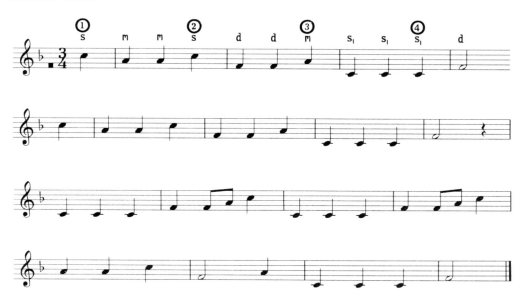

This round can be either played or sung. If you want words for it, invite the class to make some up to fit the rhythms, but you can also usefully sing the tune to its sol-fa syllables. You may need to explain what a post-horn was.

10 Music and Activities for the Second Pupils' Book

It may well be that you have spent the previous school year in working through the material in the first Pupils' Book, in which case some of the teaching points given there about pitch and rhythm will need revision after the summer break. This can be done by asking the children to look back at some of the songs in the first book that they learnt before. But remember that over-insistence on technical details can destroy children's interest in music; enthusiasm is even more important at this stage than skill. In any case many of the same teaching points will be found in the second book, though usually with a different application. As before, we have included many opportunities for the playing of classroom instruments, and again there is a set of work cards for the use of individuals or small groups. No particular time has been specified for their use, but we hope that you will have them in fairly constant operation; the children should work without close supervision, though they will sometimes need to be given simple materials such as paper, pencils, or instruments. The cards deal with rather more specific problems of pitch and rhythm than did the previous set.

The Birds' Wedding

Pupils' Book p. 2

German Folk-Song

Translated by Roger Fiske

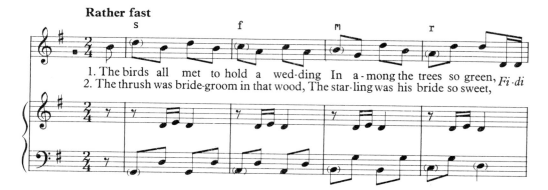

1. The birds all met to hold a wed-ding In a-mong the trees so green, *Fi·di*
2. The thrush was bride-groom in that wood, The star-ling was his bride so sweet,

ra - la - la, fi - di ra - la - la, fi - di ra - la - la - la - la - la.

3. The lark, the lark to church did bring
   The bride and all her bridesmaids neat.

4. The little tit, the little tit
   Did sing the kyrie* so sweet.

5. The little finch, the little finch
   She led them home along the street.

6. Old Mrs. Hen, old Mrs. Hen
   Kissed every guest that she did meet.

7. The cock, he crowed 'Good night, good night,
   I hope you've had enough to eat.'

* pronounced kee-ree-ay

This is a bright song and it needs sparkling singing and crisp consonants. Try singing it through yourself before teaching it to the children, and notice just how you form the consonants; thinking about this will help you to improve their quality. In the refrain 'ralala' should be sung with a short 'a' on the quavers.

Teach the song first without any accompaniment. If you want to be sure of keeping the pitch constant, have a xylophone in front of you with the notes G A B C D, and play the bracketed notes in the melody as you sing. These notes can also be used for sol-fa practice by the class. The bracketed notes in the bass make an adequate if sparse accompaniment, and they can be played on a bass xylophone, or on a cello if one is available. More expert players can expand the bass part by playing the two lower notes in every bar (the first and last notes in the final bar), and if this is successful they can then try playing the first three notes in each bar, and finally all four. The xylophone player will need two beaters. The complete accompaniment is for piano, but there is no reason why other instruments should not play as well.

Taken on their own, the bracketed notes on the top stave make a modest tune that has possibilities for development:

You can play or sing this as a round, in as many as four parts if you wish. The voices should enter at two-bar intervals, and it will not matter if some of the notes clash or are doubled by two parts. You can also make up words about birds to fit this tune; one simple sentence in the right rhythm will do, and you can use the bass printed with the original song as accompaniment.

The Pancake

Pupils' Book p. 4

Mix a pancake,
Stir a pancake,
 Pop it in a pan;
Fry the pancake,
Toss the pancake,
 Catch it if you can!

Christina Rossetti

Old Aunt Kate

Pupils' Book p. 5

American Song

Moderately fast

Old Aunt Kate she

Old Aunt Kate she bake a cake, She bake it 'hind the gar - den gate, She

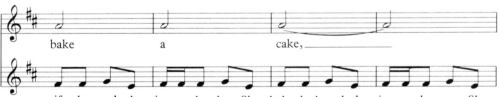

bake a cake,

sift the meal, she gim-me the dust, She bake the bread, she gim-me the crust, She

Old Aunt Kate, That's the way she took me in!

eat the meat, she gim-me the skin, And that's the way she took me in!

This short song is primarily for fun. The upper stave is optional, and should not be taught until the melody on the lower stave is known very well. The song is so short that it will not stand endless repetition. Teach the melody line and then drop the song for a while; when you come back to it you can add the upper part.

You can also use the words on their own. Say them to the children in the rhythm of the song, with great expression and at an energetic pace; twice through without a break will seem just long enough. When the children can say them as well as you can, with a very expressive rise and fall that shows just how mean Aunt Kate really is, try the words as a four-part round. Alternatively get the children to suggest a vocal accompaniment of a new kind. What does it feel like to watch someone baking when you are hungry? What sounds would you make if you thought someone was just about to put a meal in front of you? What sounds would you make if you thought this and then they didn't? Explore hungry sounds, full sounds, empty sounds, pleasure sounds, disgust sounds. Make them into a pattern, and while you say the words of the original song the children can repeat their patterns as an accompaniment.

Here is a piece by Alastair Reid called 'Sounds' (Pupils' Book p. 6):

PLOO
is breaking your shoelace.

MRRAAOWL
is what cats really say.

TRIS-TRAS
is scissors cutting paper.

KINCLUNK
is a car going over a manhole.

CROOMB
is what pigeons murmur to themselves.

PHLOOPH
is sitting suddenly on a cushion.

NYO-NYO
is speaking with your mouth full.

HARROWOLLOWORRAH
is yawning.

PALOOP
is the tap dripping in the bath.

RAM TAM PICKAGEE
is feeling good.

114

This poem is for fun. Don't destroy it by being serious about it. But you could also make your own 'sounds' piece which would involve some very serious and analytical listening.

The Riddle

Pupils' Book p. 7

German Folk-Song

Translated by Elizabeth Fiske

1. A lit - tle man is stand - ing with - in the wood;
2. The lit - tle man is si - lent and makes no sound;

He wears a pur - ple cloak and a small black hood.
He stands with on - ly one foot up - on the ground.

Tell me, tell me, if you can, What's the name of this small man,
Tell me who this man can be, For he will not an - swer me,

In a pur-ple cloak__ and a small black hood?
Stand-ing there with one__ foot up - on the ground.

This folk-song is introduced by Humperdinck into his opera *Hansel and Gretel*. The answer to the riddle is usually thought to be a toadstool; but it could equally well be the wild flower known as 'Lords and Ladies'.

The Robin and the Wren

Pupil's Book p. 4

The robin and the redbreast,
 The robin and the wren,
If you take them out of their nest,
 Ye'll ne'er thrive again.

The robin and the redbreast,
 The martin and the swallow;
If you touch one of their eggs,
 Ill luck is sure to follow.

Anon

116

The Farmer's Daughter

Pupils' Book pp. 8 & 9

English Folk-Song

1. A farmer he lived in the west coun-trie, ⎫
2. One day they did walk by the ri-ver's brim, ⎭ *Bow down, bow down,*

A farmer he lived in the west coun-trie,___ And he had daugh-ters one two and three,
One day they did walk by the ri-ver's brim, And the eld-est pushed the youngest one in,

Sing-ing I will be true un-to my love, If my love will be true un-to me.

3. 'Oh sister, oh sister, pray give me your hand,
   And I'll give you both house and land.'

4. 'I'll neither lend you hand nor glove,
   Unless you'll promise me your true love.'

5. So down the river the maiden swam
   Until she came to the miller's dam.

6. The miller's daughter stood at the door,
   Blooming like a gillyflower.

7. 'Oh father, oh father, here swims a swan,
   Very much like a gentlewoman.'

8. The miller he took his rod and hook
   And he fished the maiden out of the brook.

The essence of this song lies in the vitality of the melody, and in the rhythmic impulse that comes from the recurring chorus phrases. But there are many verses, and the song will sound monotonous unless variety of some kind is introduced. Divide the class into three groups, with each group singing two of the verses; the first and last verses should be sung by everyone, as should all the refrains. The refrain which begins with the word 'Singing' must be joined onto the preceding words with especial care; a gap here would break the rhythm.

Polish Dance Tune

Pupils' Book p. 9

Fairly fast

Soldier, Soldier

Pupils' Book pp. 10 & 11

American Folk-Song

'Sol-dier, sol-dier, won't you mar-ry me, With your mus-ket, fife and drum?'

Fine

'How can I mar-ry such a pret-ty girl as you,   shoes
                               When I've got no socks to put on?'
                               pants
          (last time) With a wife and ba-by at home?'

               Cob - blers
Off to the Dra - pers she did go, as fast as she could run.
               Tai - lors

D.C.

Brought him back the fi-nest that was there, and the sol-dier put them on.

This is a pentatonic song that may be more familiar to you in another version. Like 'Old Aunt Kate', it makes an effective word piece. Divide the class into two groups, one for the soldier and one for the unfortunate girl. Explore the use of word ostinati, that is, of words repeated over and over again in a steady rhythm; for instance, words in crotchet rhythm such as 'March, march', 'left, right', or words mainly in quaver rhythm such as 'won't you marry me', 'musket, fife, and drum'. Do not try to use all of these at once. Vary the dynamics from *pp* or even whispers to *ff*. Use spoken words to provide a rhythmic introduction and postlude to the song; the latter can suggest the soldier marching away into the distance.

When you come to teach the song, many of the above speech effects can be repeated. Here are two fragments that can be either played or sung as an accompaniment:

If you would prefer other words you will need other rhythms and perhaps other notes. Do not devise these yourself, but leave the choice to a small group of children. Send them away with pitched instruments, and they may well come back with ideas that had not occurred to you.

Kukuriku

Pupils' Book p. 12

Israeli Round

English text by Schwartz and Kevers

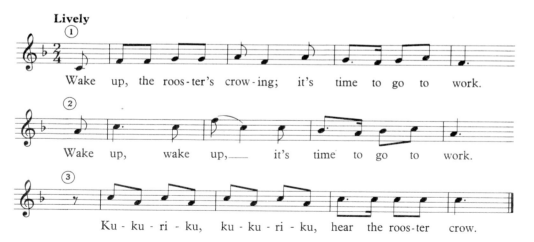

By the nature of the words, this round cannot be sung slowly. Here is a plan for teaching it.
1. Sing the round through twice to the class, at a brisk pace with lively words and expression.
2. Sing line 1 using your hands to indicate the rise and fall of the melody; repeat immediately with the children joining in.
3. Sing line 2 and repeat with the children.
4. Sing lines 1 and 2 and repeat with the children.
5. Sing line 3 and repeat with the children.
6. Sing the whole round and repeat with the children.

The process from 2 onwards should be completed without breaking the rhythm. No verbal explanation should be necessary; all that is needed can be done with the singing voice and the hands.

Now ask the class to sing it without your help. Give a starting note and count two. Next, divide the class into two, asking each half to sing the round in turn. If this is satisfactory, make three groups, each group singing in turn. If you think the learning process has now lasted long enough, leave the round for the time being. But if the class is still fresh, try it first in two parts and then in three.

The fine painting of a cock is by Picasso (Pupils' Book p. 12).

The Little Dove

Czech Folk-Song

Translated by Roger Fiske

1. Once a lit - tle dove flew off a rock so steep, rock so steep,
2. If the blue-eyed maid-en had-n't slept so sound, slept so sound,

And it woke the blue - eyed maid - en from her sleep.
She'd have caught the lit - tle dove up - on the ground.

A useful song for revising the top notes of the sol-fa ladder. Do not take it too fast; the
scale and arpeggio passages are hard to sing in tune except at a very moderate pace.

Fais Dodo

Pupils' Book p. 13

French Lullaby

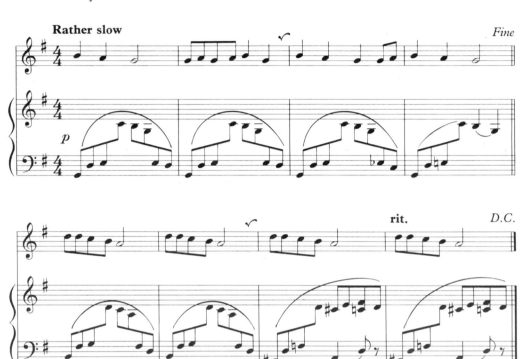

The Holly and the Ivy Pupils' Book pp. 14 & 15

English Carol

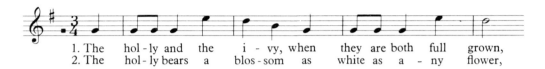

1. The hol-ly and the i-vy, when they are both full grown,
2. The hol-ly bears a blos-som as white as a-ny flower,

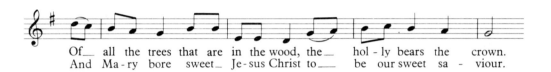

Of all the trees that are in the wood, the hol-ly bears the crown.
And Ma-ry bore sweet Je-sus Christ to be our sweet sa-viour.

The ris-ing of the sun and the run-ning of the deer,

The play-ing of the mer-ry or-gan, sweet sing-ing in the choir.

3. The holly bears a berry as red as any blood,
   And Mary bore sweet Jesus Christ to do poor sinners good.

4. The holly bears a prickle as sharp as any thorn,
   And Mary bore sweet Jesus Christ on Christmas Day in the morn.

5. The holly and the ivy, when they are both full grown,
   Of all the trees that are in the wood the holly bears the crown.

This well-known carol has been arranged for simple two-part singing. The lower part consists mainly of a downward and upward scale passage, and it should not prove too difficult to children who have had experience in singing rounds. The tune should first be taught to everyone. When the children know it, you can join in with the lower part. Finally let half the children sing the top line and half the bottom line. Make sure that the high notes in bars 1 and 3 of the tune are not flat, and don't forget the pause (⌢) in the last bar.

A melody gets its character from the rise and fall of the notes and from the contrast between long notes and short ones. The character of holly comes from its spiky shape whereas ivy is winding and sinuous. Draw on the board a holly branch and an ivy trail. Ask the children to describe how they differ, and ask them also how they think the difference could be expressed in sound. The spiky sounds will be easy, but the winding ones will need more imagination. Divide the children into groups, preferably with not more than five to a group. Provide each group with a mixture of pitched and unpitched instruments, not forgetting recorders and piano. Ask for group compositions about holly and ivy. Go round the groups advising on the shape of the compositions. This is not an easy task. What is shape, in terms of music? It may mean four matching phrases, or it may mean a simple rise and fall like an arch. What shapes do holly and ivy make in nature? When the children have finished, the pieces should be performed.

The Tarantella from Respighi's *La Boutique Fantasque* (no. 8 on the tape) illustrates the contrast agreeably.

Bye Bye Baby　　　　　Pupils' Book p. 15

Appalachian Lullaby

The Old Man of the Woods

Pupils' Book p. 16

Welsh Folk-Song

Words by Anne Mendoza

1. Chop-ping trees and cut-ting bran-ches,
2. Trees for Christ-mas, tall or short ones,
3. Come and buy now, all good peo-ple,

In the wood there is an old man,
In the wood the old man's chop-ping,
From the old man in the wood,

In the wood there is an old man,
In the wood the old man's chop-ping
From the old man in the wood,

Chop-ping trees and cut -ting bran - ches.
Trees for Christ - mas, tall or short ones.
Come and buy now, all good peo - ple.

This is a secular Christmas song. The accompaniment can be for piano, or for classroom instruments, or for a mixture of the two, and it should suggest the rhythmic movement of chopping, with one swing to each bar. Experiment with a variety of instruments, and encourage the children to suggest which they think would be most effective. We have printed the bass part on the first beat of each bar, with chords on the second and third beats, but you might prefer the other way round, with a chord on the first beat and the bass notes on the second and third beats; or chords on the first and third beats, and the bass notes on the second.

When you walk in the woods you often hear more than you actually see. The picture (Pupils' Book p. 17) is of woods, but you cannot see the woodcutter.

Children Go, I Will Send You

American Carol from Harlem

Pupils' Book pp. 18 & 19

Leader
Chil-dren go, I will send you.

Chorus
How will you send me?

Leader
1. Oh I will send you one by one,
2. Oh I will send you two by two,

Chorus *Repeat for later verses*
One for the lit-tle bit-ty ba-by
Two for Jo-seph and Ma-ry

boy Born in Beth-le-hem, Beth-le-

-hem, Beth-le-hem.

3. Three for the good old wise men.

4. Four for the ox-en that stood in the stall,

5. Five for the snow that lay on the ground.

6. Six for the stars that shone in the sky,
    Five for the snow that lay on the ground,
    Four for the oxen that stood in the stall,
    Three for the good old wise men,
    Two for Joseph and Mary,
    One for the little bitty baby boy
    Born in Bethlehem, Bethlehem, Bethlehem.

This cumulative carol is sung like 'The Twelve Days of Christmas' or 'Green Grow the Rushes O'. Like all cumulative songs, it is easier to sing than to explain.

It has no accompaniment and must be sung with an energetic swing. The rhythms of verses 4, 5, and 6 are only approximate.

A picture of a star appears with this carol (Pupils' Book p. 18). The stars are mysterious and beautiful and might suggest a number of related ideas.

To Bethlehem

Spanish Dance Carðl

Translated by Peter D. Smith

Spirited

1. Down to Beth -le -hem the shep -herds run in ce -le -bra - tion
Of the birth of him whose life means hope for ev -ery na - tion.

Ay! Ay! Ay! with the pipe and the drum, the gui -tar is mer-ri -ly strum -ming, The

shep-herds hap-pi -ly run -ning.

2. Soon they come down to the manger which the Christ was born in,
   Greeting him with songs and dancing on that happy morning.

3. From that day the word of Jesus has been penetrating
   Through the world, which has so long for love and hope been waiting.

4. Come and join us in this dance and fill the world with singing.
   Jesus calls the tune that changes us, a new life bringing.

This carol suggests various kinds of accompaniment. The printed bass part can be played on a bass xylophone and can easily be taught by rote. Certain notes will need adaptation by playing them an octave higher; the last two bars need special attention in this way.

A rhythmic pattern seems called for. Perhaps one verse could be decorated with clapping, stamping, or untuned percussion.

The right-hand part of the piano accompaniment can also be played an octave higher. This will mean that the sung melody will sound below the piano melody, giving a fresh effect.

Past Three O'Clock

Pupils' Book p. 21

English Carol

Past three o'-clock, And a cold frost-y morn - ing.

Past three o'-clock, Good mor-row mas-ters all.

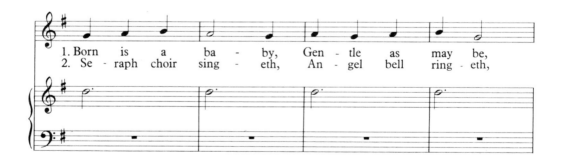

1. Born is a ba - by, Gen-tle as may be,
2. Se - raph choir sing - eth, An - gel bell ring - eth,

Son of the e-ter - nal Fa - ther su - per - nal.
Hark how they rhyme it, Time it and chime it.

3. Cheese from the dairy bring they for Mary,
   And, not for money, butter and honey,

4. Light out of starland leadeth from far land
   Princes to meet him, worship and greet him.

The lower stave of the accompaniment is for piano or bass xylophone or cello. The upper stave is for three recorders, each player taking a note in each chord; thus each player has three different notes to play.

Begin the carol with only the bass notes, and add one recorder in each chorus:

Chorus 1: Bass only
Chorus 2: Add lowest recorder
Chorus 3: Add middle recorder
Chorus 4: Add highest recorder

In the verses a single instrument will be sufficient.

The idea of accompanying a melody with a repeated note pattern is very old, and many composers have used it. A repeated note pattern very like the one in this carol was used by Bizet in the 'Carillon' from his suite, *L'Arlésienne* (no. 9 on the tape), where it is meant to sound like church bells.

The Nightwatchman picture (Pupils' Book p. 21) reminds the children that the chorus of the song is about something that really happened. It is interesting to think how the function of nightwatchmen has changed.

The Cradle

Austrian Carol

Translated by Robert Graves

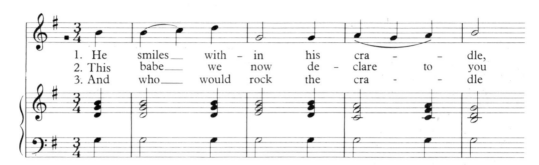

1. He smiles__ with-in his cra - dle,
2. This babe__ we now de-clare to you
3. And who__ would rock the cra - dle

A babe with face__ so bright,_____
Is Je-sus Christ__ the Lord;_____
Where-in this in-fant lies,_____

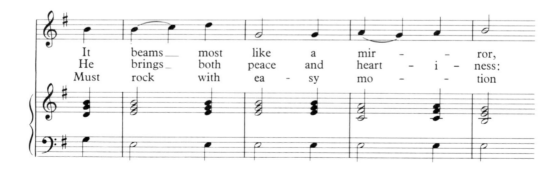

It beams__ most like a mir - - ror,
He brings__ both peace and heart - i - ness:
Must rock with ea - sy mo - - tion

Take this carol rather slowly and quietly. You must listen hard and watch the children's faces to make sure that the flow of the melody is not being broken by too frequent breaths.

Welsh Lullaby Pupils' Book p. 23

Sur le Pont d'Avignon

Pupils' Book p. 24

French Song

Sur le pont d'Avignon
On y danse, on y danse,
Sur le pont d'Avignon
On y danse tout en rond.

On the bridge at Avignon
They are dancing, they are dancing,
On the bridge at Avignon
They are dancing round and round.

1. Les beaux messieurs font comme ça,
   Et puis encore comme ça.

   The gentlemen go like this,
   Then they all go like this.

2. Les belles dames font comme ça,
   Et puis encore comme ça.

   The ladies they go like this,
   Then they all go like this.

3. Les musiciens font comme ça,
   Et puis encore comme ça.

   The musicians they go like this,
   Then they all go like this.

4. Les soldats font comme ça,
   Et puis encore comme ça.

   The soldiers they go like this,
   Then they all go like this.

If you sing this song in English, verse 3 will have to begin with two quick notes on the upbeat. But we hope you will prefer the original French words, which cannot be adequately translated. This is a song about dancing, and it should be sung lightly, though not too fast, to preserve the feeling of the dance. No dance song should really be sung sitting down, but if you lack the space for the children to skip round in a circle, let their fingers and hands dance as an accompaniment. In bars 10 and 12 there are pauses to allow for suitable movement. Ask the children for suggestions as to what these movements should be. In each verse they can either repeat the same movement or devise two different ones.

The accompaniment is for piano, but with small alterations it can be played on class-room instruments. The top stave can be played an octave down on a glockenspiel. The bottom stave would sound well on a metallophone, or chime bars could be used. In the latter case the Bs in bars 1, 5, and 8 will have to be left out. In bars 9–12 a bass xylophone will provide contrast, but a cello will sustain the notes better; leave out the high notes in these bars if you are not using a piano.

Swedish Folk Tune

The Judge's Dance

Pupils' Book p. 25

W   Pupils' Book p. 25

The King sent for his wise men all
    To find a rhyme for W.
When they had thought for a good long time
But could not think of a single rhyme,
    'I'm sorry', said he, 'to trouble you'.

                                        James Reeves

At Avignon apparently *everybody* danced on the bridge. But why should a judge dance in Sweden?

The Keeper

Pupils' Book pp. 26 & 27

English Folk-Song

1. The keep - er did a - shoot - ing go, And
2. The first doe he shot at he missed, The
3. The fourth doe she did cross the plain; The

un - der his coat he car - ried a bow All for to shoot at a
sec - ond doe he trimmed, he kissed, The third doe went where
keep - er fetched her back a - gain. Where she is now she

mer - ry lit - tle doe A - mong the leaves so green O.
no - bo - dy wist A - mong the leaves so green O.
may re - main A - mong the leaves so green O.

A   B   A   B   A   B
Jac - kie Boy! Mas - ter! Sing ye well! Ve - ry well! Hey down, Ho down,

A   Both   A
Der - ry der - ry down, A - mong the leaves so green O. To my

B   A   B
hey down down, To my ho down down, Hey down, Ho down,

A   Both
Der - ry der - ry down, A - mong the leaves so green O.

This folk-song comes from Warwickshire, and it is best sung unaccompanied. Explain very briefly what a gamekeeper does, though the one in the song in fact sounds more like a poacher.

Once the song has been learnt by everyone, it can be sung in groups, one group singing the phrases marked A and the other those marked B. You will have to work hard to maintain the rhythm in these passages, but we must emphasize that the feeling for the rhythm will come from the way you sing the song initially, and from the precision with which you bring in each group.

This and the next three songs have two things in common. The first is that they are all English folk-songs collected by Cecil Sharp. Cecil Sharp (1859–1924) was the most important of all English folk-song collectors. From about 1900 onwards he was wandering round the villages of England, but most often in Somerset, asking the old people to sing him the songs they had learnt from their parents. He wrote these songs down, tune and words, and had them printed with his own piano accompaniments. But for him many of these songs would have been forgotten and lost for ever. Many of them are hundreds of years old, and nobody knows who made them up. Sometimes they were made up to commemorate something that had actually happened: for instance 'High Germany' and 'The Farmer's Daughter'. They passed from village to village, becoming changed in small details as people forgot a word here and a note there and had to invent something of their own instead. That is why collectors have often found several versions of the same folk-song, and nobody can say which one is the original. Sometimes the same folk tune seems to survive in several countries. For instance 'Rocking' from Czechoslovakia, and 'Paul's Little Hen', which is popular in all Scandinavian countries, seem to be close relatives of our own 'Baa, Baa, Black Sheep'; they may all have a common origin.

Needless to say, this information should not all be passed on to the children. But there are so many folk-songs in this book that it seemed important to say something about their origin and characteristics. Perhaps it should be added that the English 'Traditional Song' is not usually a folk-song; in all probability it is the work of a more-or-less trained musician whose name we have forgotten. For instance 'Sweet Polly Oliver' and 'High Germany' may date from the same eighteenth-century war, but whereas the former has a sophisticated charm, needs an accompaniment, and exists in only one version, the latter is unsophisticated and heart-felt, needs no accompaniment, and exists in several versions.

These distinctions have become blurred in the last few years, for the term folk-song is now used for any newly-composed song in the folk idiom. In that such songs refer to contemporary events and are direct in their musical language, they have something in common with the folk-songs of the past.

'The Keeper' and the next three songs are also alike in that they all contain the rhythm

Sweet Nightingale

Pupils' Book pp. 28 & 29

English Folk-Song

1. My sweet-heart, come a - long, Don't you hear the sweet song,
2. Pret - ty Bet - ty, don't fail, For I'll car - ry the pail

The sweet notes of the night - in - gale flow?
Safe home to your cot as we go.

Don't you hear the fond tale Of the sweet night - in - gale
You shall

As she sings in the val-ley be-low,

As she sings in the val-ley be-low.

3. Pray let me alone;
   I have hands of my own.
   Along with you, sir, I'll not go
   To hear the fond tale, etc.

4. Pray sit yourself down
   With me on the ground,
   On this bank where the primroses grow;
   You shall hear the fond tale, etc.

5. The couple agreed,
   And were married with speed,
   And soon to the church they did go.
   No more is she afraid
   For to walk in the shade,
   Nor to sit in those valleys below,
   Nor to sit in those valleys below.

'The Keeper' and the next three songs are also alike in that they all contain the rhythm

taa - a - té

This dotted rhythm has occurred in one or two of the earlier songs, but attention has not been drawn to it until now. In 'Sweet Nightingale' the dotted rhythm  appears within a framework of three beats:

taa - a - té taa   taa - a - té taa

In the next two songs, as in 'The Keeper', it appears within a framework of four beats:

taa - a - té taa   taa   taa - a - té taa   taa

Let the children experience the feel of these rhythms by clapping them.

Here is a rhythm round which we will call the 'Pony Round', because it uses various hoof-beat patterns. It can be clapped, or played on unpitched instruments. Teach it first by rote. When it is thoroughly learnt, write it on the board. Note that the third and fourth groups sound alike, but look different.

The round can be played slowly at first, but it will be more interesting when it goes quickly.

Blow Away the Morning Dew Pupils' Book p. 29

English Folk-Song from Somerset

High Germany

Pupils' Book pp. 30 & 31

English Folk-Song

In strict march time

1. O Pol - ly love, O Pol - ly, the rout has now be - gun,
2. O Bil - ly, my dear Bil - ly, lis - ten to what I say,

And we must march a - way at the beat - ing of _ the drum;
My _ feet they are _ so ve - ry sore, I can - not march a - way;

Go _ dress your - self all _ in your best and come a - long with me,
Be - sides, my dear - est _ Bil - ly, I am with child by thee,

I'll take you to the cru - el wars in High _ Ger - ma - ny.
I am not fit for cru - el wars in High _ Ger - ma - ny.

3. I'll buy a horse for you, my love; my Polly, you shall ride,
   And all my heart's delight shall be a-walking by your side.
   We'll call at every ale-house that ever we pass by—
   We'll sweetheart on the road, my love, get married by and by.

4. O cruel, cruel was the war when first the rout began,
   And out of Old England went many a smart young man.
   They pressed my love away from me, likewise my brothers three,
   They sent them to the war, my love, in High Germany.

5. The drum that my love's beating is covered all in green.
   The pretty lambs are sporting, 'tis pleasure to be seen,
   And when my pretty babe is born, sits smiling on my knee,
   I'll think upon my own true love in High Germany.

These are the words Cecil Sharp collected at the beginning of this century; when publishing the song for the schools of his day, he altered them considerably. You will have to explain what pressgangs did in the eighteenth century (see verse 4 line 3).

There are two beats to the bar; as an introduction play the LH drone in bar 1 four times, once on each beat (or minim). The imitation bugle calls in the accompaniment stress that this song is a march.

The picture (Pupils' Book p.31) is of Ensign Macdougal of the Hopetoun Fencibles in 1795.

This and the next song occur without their words in the March, 'Folk-songs from Somerset', the last movement of Vaughan Williams's *English Folk-song Suite* (no. 10 on the tape). Originally this suite was composed for military band; it has been arranged for orchestra by Gordon Jacob. The March begins with the tune given on page 143, 'Blow away the Morning Dew', and it is in ABA form:

A has 2 tunes: Blow away the Morning Dew
                High Germany
B has 2 tunes: Whistle, Daughter, Whistle
                John Barleycorn
A is then repeated.

'High Germany' is played very much faster than it should be sung. 'John Barleycorn' comes in the bass, and the children may at first find it hard to hear.

John Barleycorn

Pupils' Book pp. 32 & 33

English Folk-Song

Not too fast and very rhythmic

1. There came three men from out the west Their vic-tor-y__ to try,
2. They took a plough and ploughed him in, Laid clods up-on_ his head,

staccato

And they have ta-ken a sol-emn oath John Bar-ley-corn should die.____
And they have ta-ken a sol-emn oath John Bar-ley-corn is dead.__

Sing ri-fol-lol, the did-dle all the dee, Right fal-lee-ro-dee.

3. So then he lay for three long weeks
   Till dew from heaven did fall.
   John Barleycorn sprang up again,
   And that surprised them all.

4. There he remained till midsummer,
   And looked both pale and wan,
   For all he had a spiky beard
   To show he was a man.

5. But soon men came with their sharp scythes
   And chopped him to the knee;
   They rolled and tied him by the waist
   And served him barbarously.

This song has four beats to the bar, and should sound solid and almost ponderous. The words are about the sowing and reaping of corn, and they will remind country children of harvest. Few children will have seen corn cut by hand. The picture of the combine harvester (Pupils' Book p. 33) is a reminder of the change. Develop ideas about harvest in the country and about autumn. How do town children know that autumn has come? What can they see which tells them it is harvest time? For the country child the sight of corn being cut and the sound of the combine harvester are the signs of harvest, but in the cities it may be that the factory is the substitute for the field. This may show no seasonal change and perhaps the dress shop with its autumn display will be the only reminder, unless there is a nearby park.

You could do some interesting rhythm work about autumn and harvesting. Each child should be allotted some means of making a sound—a pitched or unpitched classroom instrument, a recorder or recorder top, two pencils to click together, a ruler to twang on the desk; some children could make voiced clicks and pops with their mouths. Go round the class beating a four beat rhythm and ask for each sound in turn on the beats. This may result at first in laughter and near-chaos, but keep trying various combinations of different sounds; later you can vary the tempo and ask for the dotted rhythm that comes in 'Sweet Nightingale' and more recent songs. Now send the children off in groups to make sound patterns about a combine harvester or a factory. You may be able to build what they come back with into a larger feature about growth, ripening, and harvest, perhaps bringing in poetry, movement, and pictures.

Hill an' Gully

Jamaican Song

Hill an' Gul-ly ride - a, Hill an' Gul-ly.

Hill an' Gul-ly ride - a, Hill an' Gul-ly.

An' a ben dung low dung, Hill an' Gul-ly.

An' a low dung bes-sy dung, Hill an' Gul-ly.

An' yuh bet-ter min' yuh tum-ble dung, Hill an' Gul-ly.

A marvellously rhythmic song. 'Dung' means 'down', but it would be a waste of time to bother too much about the meaning of the words. Don't use the tune for rhythm reading; many West Indian tunes are too subtle for exact notation. The class will learn more from the way you sing it.

Use rhythm instruments for the accompaniment—wood blocks, claves, drums tapped with the fingers. First ask the children to play quite simply in minims (two beats to the bar), crotchets (four beats), or quavers (eight beats), but not all at once; you might, for instance, sing the song three times with a different rhythm in the accompaniment each time; or three times starting with minims for verse 1, adding crotchets for verse 2 and quavers for verse 3. Later the children can find more complex rhythms to play in the tune itself; the rhythm of bar 1 for instance could be repeated throughout the song. Where possible, let the children choose what rhythm to play.

As an introduction tap four crotchet beats, and do not forget to give the singers their starting note.

Que Venez-Vous Chercher?

French Folk Dance

Pupils' Book p. 35

or continue L.H. as in bars 1—4

Serbian Folk Tune

Pupils' Book p. 35

Ukrainian Dance Song Pupils' Book p. 36

When I First Came to this Land Pupils' Book p. 37

American Song

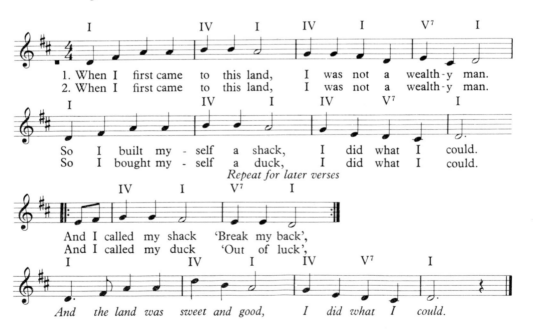

1. When I first came to this land, I was not a wealth-y man.
2. When I first came to this land, I was not a wealth-y man.

So I built my-self a shack, I did what I could.
So I bought my-self a duck, I did what I could.

Repeat for later verses

And I called my shack 'Break my back',
And I called my duck 'Out of luck',

And the land was sweet and good, I did what I could.

3. And I called my donkey 'Horse gone wonky',

4. And I called my wife 'Run for your life',

The song hardly needs teaching. Just sing it to the children and encourage them to join in when they wish; even when they know it, they may prefer to sing only the choruses, with the teacher alone singing the verses. It is fun to get faster and faster in the last verse up to the words 'And the land was sweet and good', and then slow down for a broad ending. The chord symbols may be used for guitar, but the song is just as effective with no accompaniment at all.

Heave Away

Pupils' Book p. 38

Cornish Shanty

Some-times we're bound for Liv-er-pool town, Sometimes we're bound for

France. Heave a - way, __ O my John - ny, Heave a - way. __

__ Some-times we're bound for Liv-er-pool town, Sometimes we're bound for

France. Heave a - way, __ O my jol - ly boys, We're all bound to go. __

This shanty has only one verse. Others have been added in the past, but they do not seem particularly suitable and we have not printed them. Such a short song needs more verses so there is a chance for the children to invent some, perhaps of local significance. But they will not be able to do so until they are thoroughly familiar with the tune of the first verse.

The Grey Hawk

Pupils' Book p. 39

English Folk-Song

1. Once I had a grey hawk, and a pret - ty grey hawk,
2. It's o'er the wide fo - rest I ram - bled a - way,

A sweet pret - ty bird of my own.
And through the green fields I did stray.

But she took a flight, She flew a - way quite,
I hul - loa'd, I whooped, I played on my flute;

And there's no - bo - dy knows where she's gone, my brave boys,
Not my sweet pret - ty bird could I find, my brave boys,

And there's no - bo - dy knows where she's gone. ____
Not my sweet pret - ty bird could I find. ____

This song comes from Dorset. The introduction is best taken from the last four bars. It will be worth your while to give rather more attention than usual to the way this song is performed. It needs very smooth ('legato') singing, and the long tied notes must last for their full length. Some of the phrases are long, some quite short, and the children should practise taking breath between the phrases and not in the middle of them. As in so many songs, you can tell where a phrase ends from the sense of the words as well as from the sense of the tune. Here each printed line represents a phrase.

There have been several songs about birds in this book. It is natural that they should attract the folk poet and song maker, for, living in the country, he is surrounded by bird-song every day of his life, and occasionally he will hear birds at night as well. Ask the children to think of as many kinds of birdsong as they can. They will probably know the sound of a cuckoo, and just possibly that of an owl. Tell them of other birdsongs. Do some birds make music while others make only noise? Even in towns you can sometimes hear the very quick tk-tk-tk-tk of a blackbird when alarmed, and you may be lucky enough to hear it sing as well. If your school is in a suitable locality, take the children outside and listen to whatever birds may be around. Back in the classroom, discuss with the children how they would make various bird calls on instruments, and then get them to build up a dawn chorus; they can use recorder tops, whistles, glockenspiels, voices. Use a cymbal beaten with a soft stick to give an impression of sunrise, and then start with a cock crow and gradually build up to a climax. Record the piece on tape and listen to it with the children. Was it music or just noise?

Many composers have imitated birdsong. Let the children listen to the extract from *Chronochromie* by the modern French composer, Messiaen (no. 11 on the tape); the passage consists entirely of bird calls he heard in one country or another, played on strings. The children may also enjoy *The Cuckoo* by another modern French composer, Milhaud (no. 12); it is an arrangement of an old tune for wind instruments.

Springtime   Pupils' Book p. 40

Hark, the Bells   Pupils' Book p. 40

Moritz Hauptmann; words by Imogen Holst

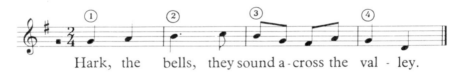

Hark, the   bells, they sound a-cross the val - ley.

Bar 3 is not easy; indicate the relative pitches of the notes, and take it slowly.

Like so many rounds, this one is based on two chords in alternation, tonic and dominant. You and the children should be able to make up a similar round for yourselves, beginning with one in two parts. Invent a sentence that will fit four bars of $\frac{2}{4}$ time, as in 'Hark, the Bells'. For example:

School   is   o - ver   for   to - day.

Now for the tune. For the first beat of each bar choose a note from the tonic chord of G major:

and for the second beat of each bar a note from the dominant (D major), with the addition of the 7th, written here in brackets:

Make sure that your tune flows smoothly without jumping all over the place. Here is an example:

Not a brilliant piece, but a starting point. By experiment you will be able to find more interesting series of notes. When you have achieved a satisfactory two-part round, try one in four parts; you will often find that a two-part round works in four parts just as well.

Eastertide

Dutch Carol

Translated by Jack Dobbs

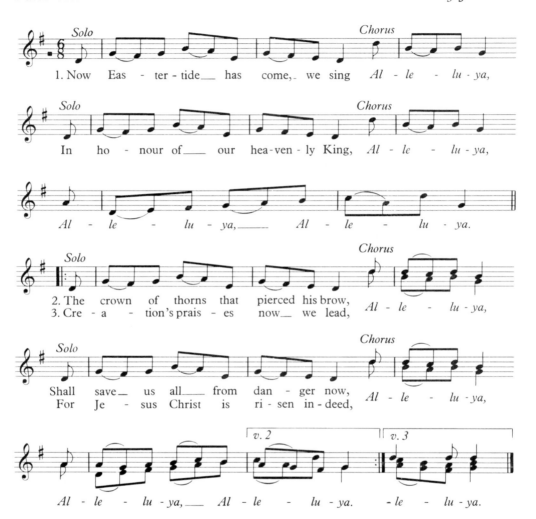

1. Now Eas - ter - tide__ has come,_ we sing Al - le - lu - ya,
In ho - nour of__ our hea - ven - ly King, Al - le - lu - ya,
Al - le - lu - ya,___ Al - le - lu - ya.

2. The crown of thorns that pierced his brow,
3. Cre - a - tion's prais - es now__ we lead, Al - le - lu - ya,

Shall save__ us all__ from dan - ger now,
For Je - sus Christ is ri - sen in - deed, Al - le - lu - ya,

Al - le - lu - ya,__ Al - le - lu - ya. - le - lu - ya.

This Easter carol should be taught as a unison song (verse 1 only). Beat an easy two beats in the bar, and keep the music flowing. The later verses have been arranged for two-part singing, the original tune being written with the stems down and the additional part with the stems up; notice that the additional part is not always above the tune. The phrases marked 'Solo' can be sung by a small group, or even by a solo voice if you have one you can rely on. The two parts in the Hallelujahs will need to be learnt separately. The three-note chords at the end are optional, but if you can achieve them you will have given the children an exciting experience.

Spring Carol

Pupils' Book pp. 42 & 43

Welsh Folk-Song: Nos Galan

English words by Jack Dobbs

Gaily

lightly

1. Let us sing with hearts o'er-flow-ing, Fa, la, la, la, la, la, la, la, la.
2. Ech-o, moun-tains, with our sing-ing, Fa, la, la, la, la, la, la, la, la.

Now the win-ter's quick-ly go-ing, Fa, la, la, la, la, la, la, la, la.
Stee-ple bells, be-gin your ring-ing, Fa, la, la, la, la, la, la, la, la.

In the spring we'll show our glad-ness, Fa, la, la, la, la, la, la, la, la.
Dance we round, our gar-lands wear-ing, Fa, la, la, la, la, la, la, la.

Cast a-way all thoughts of sad-ness, Fa, la, la, la, la, la, la, la, la.
With our friends our new hopes shar-ing, Fa, la, la, la, la, la, la, la, la.

Not all carols are for use at Christmas; some of the oldest celebrate other seasons of the year as this one does. The history of the carol is fascinating, and those who wish to know more will find a clear and amusing account in the preface to *The Oxford Book of Carols*. Carols were danced as well as sung, and performances must have the feel of the dance in them. The rhythm of the piano accompaniment is meant to suggest the beating of a drum, and indeed a drum may provide sufficient accompaniment on its own. Whatever you use, keep the music light and on the move. Do not give way to what *The Oxford Book of Carols* calls 'the British tendency to lugubriousness'.

Welsh schools may prefer to sing the tune to the original words:

1. Oer yw'r gwr sy'n methu caru,
   Fa la la la la la la la la.
   Hen fynyddoedd anwyl Cymru,
   Fa la la la la la la la la.
   Iddo ef a'u câr gynhesaf,
   Fa la la la la la la la la.
   Gwyliau llawen flwyddyn nesaf,
   Fa la la la la la la la la.

2. I'r helbulus oer yw'r biliau,
   Sydd yn dyfod yn y Gwyliau,
   Gwrando bregeth mewn un pennill,
   Byth na waria fwr na'th ennill.

3. Oer yw'r eira ae Eryri,
   Er fod gwrthban gwlanen arni,
   Oer yw'r bobol na ofalan',
   Gwrdd a'u gilydd, Ar Nos Galan.

Sourwood Mountain

Pupils' Book p. 44

Appalachian Folk-Song

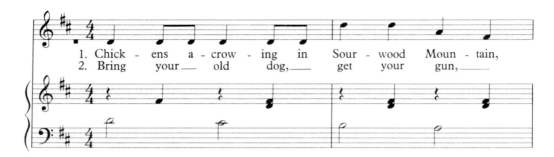

1. Chick - ens a - crow - ing in Sour - wood Moun - tain,
2. Bring your old dog, get your gun,

3. I got a gal in the head of the hollow,
   She won't come and I won't follow.

4. My true love's a blue-eyed daisy,
   She won't work and I'm too lazy.

This is one of the many songs that Cecil Sharp collected in the Appalachian Mountains of North America towards the end of his life. It is a dance song, and it should be danced as well as sung, but if this is impossible then foot tapping, off-beat clapping, and very vigorous singing will have to be a substitute. We cannot say too often or too strongly that music and movement are closely linked, sometimes in a fairly obvious way as in this song, and sometimes in a more subtle and less direct way. It is for the teacher to seek out the movement that is latent in a piece of music and to persuade the children to react to it. Your triumph will be when the children *can't* sit still.

The Wee Cooper o' Fife

Pupils' Book p. 45

Scots Folk-Song

1. There was a wee coo-per wha lived in Fife,
2. She wad - na bake, nor she wad - na brew,

Nick - e - ty, nack - e - ty, noo, noo, noo,

And he has got - ten a gen - tle wife,
For spoil - ing o' her come - ly hue,

Hey wil - ly wal - lac - ky, hoo John Dou - gal,

A - lone quo' Rush - i - ty, roue, roue, roue.

3. She wadna wash, nor she wadna wring,
   For the spoiling o' her gowden ring.

4. The cooper has gane to his woo' pack,
   And he's laid a sheep's skin on his wife's back.

5. 'It's I'll no thrash ye for your gentle kin,
   But I will thrash my ain sheep's skin.'

6. 'Oh I will bake and I will brew,
   And nae mair think o' my comely hue.'

7. A' ye wha ha'e gotten a gentle wife,
   Just you send for the wee cooper o' Fife.

o'—of; wadna—would not; gowden—golden; ain—own; nae mair—no more;
A' ye wha ha'e—All you who have

The teacher with a good Scots accent will have the advantage in this song. It should go rather fast, with crisp words and accurate tuning; watch especially the rising scale in bar 3. A cooper is a man who makes barrels, in particular beer barrels.

Words usually have a more flexible rhythm than music, but sometimes there is a kind of parallel. The following verses have the feel of the six-eight rhythm in 'The Wee Cooper o' Fife'. Read them to the children, but only as a piece of fun; mention the suggestion of a six-eight rhythm, but if you make too much of this no one will enjoy the poem.

Sink Song   Pupils' Book p. 46

Scouring out the porridge pot,
   Round and round and round!

Out with all the scraith and scoopery,
Lift the eely ooly droopery,
Chase the glubbery slubbery gloopery
   Round and round and round!

Out with all the doleful dithery,
Ladle out the slimy slithery,
Hunt and catch the hithery thithery
   Round and round and round!

Out with all the ubbly gubbly,
On the stove it burns so bubbly;
Use the spoon and use it doubly
   Round and round and round.

                    J. A. Lindon

Hush-You-Bye

Pupils' Book, p. 47

American Folk-Song

1. Hush-you-bye, Don't you cry, Go to sleep-y, lit-tle ba - by.

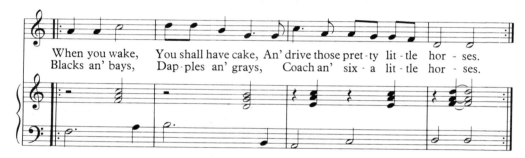

When you wake, You shall have cake, An' drive those pret-ty lit-tle hor - ses.
Blacks an' bays, Dap-ples an' grays, Coach an' six - a lit-tle hor - ses.

2. Rock-a-bye,
   Don't you cry,
   Go to sleepy, little baby.
   Send you to school
   Ridin' on a mule,
   An' drivin' those pretty little horses.
   Blacks an' bays,
   Dapples an' grays,
   Coach an' six-a little horses.

One of several versions of these words. The tune is not in a key so there is no *doh* marked at the beginning. It is instead in the Dorian mode, the notes of which are D to D' on the white notes of the piano. The accompaniment would sound very well on a metallophone for the bass part and chime bars for the chords.

The Tree on the Hill Pupils' Book pp. 48 & 49

Danish Folk-Song

Translated by John Horton

1. Deep in the for-est stood a lit-tle hill; I ne-ver saw so fine a lit-tle hill
2. On that lit-tle hill there grew a lit-tle tree; I ne-ver saw so fine a lit-tle tree,

Repeat for later verses

Tree on the hill, Stand-ing all a-lone＿＿ in the for-est.
Stand-ing all a-lone＿＿ in the for-est.

3. On that little tree there grew a little branch;

4. On that little branch there grew a little twig;

5. On that little twig there lay a little nest;

6. On that little nest there lay a little egg;

7. From that little egg there came a little bird;

8. On that little bird there grew a little down;

9. From that little down there came a little pillow;

10. On that little pillow lay a little boy;
    I never saw so fine a little boy.
    Boy on the pillow,
    Pillow from the down,
    Down on the bird,
    Bird from the egg,
    Egg in the nest,
    Nest on the twig,
    Twig on the branch,
    Branch on the tree,
    Tree on the hill,
    Standing all alone in the forest.

Another cumulative song. The feeling behind the notes is that of a lilting waltz. Sing the song through from start to finish, and see how many of the children have picked it up by the end. Once everyone knows it, it can become a test of alertness. By the end of the song nine different phrases are sung to the notes of the repeated bar, so divide the class into as many groups as you like up to nine, and then, with you singing the start of each verse, ask the groups in varying orders for each phrase in turn. Keep changing the order so that they are all on their toes. Everyone joins in each time with the last three bars.

Make sure that the tied note is held for its full length.

Orientis Partibus Pupils' Book p. 50

Old French Melody

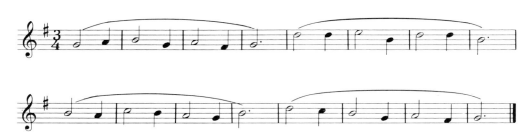

Ah, Mon Beau Château Pupils' Book p. 50

French Folk-Song

Dachshund Pupils' Book p. 51

Sharp nose raised
He centipedes by,

      Three dogs long,
      And half a dog high.

A round smooth hull
For his tail to steer,

      And two little squat legs
      Bringing up the rear.

                    Clive Sansom

The dachshund picture (Pupils' Book p. 51) is full of sounds, and your imagination will suggest many others as well.

Slowly Pupils' Book p. 52

Slowly the tide creeps up the sand,
Slowly the shadows cross the land,
Slowly the cart-horse pulls his mile,
Slowly the old man mounts the stile.

Slowly the hands move round the clock,
Slowly the dew dries on the dock.
Slow is the snail—but slowest of all
The green moss spreads on the old brick wall.

                    James Reeves

Jumbuck Skinning Man

Pupils' Book p. 53

Australian Song

Repeat chorus after each verse

2. Jumping crackers, crackerjacks,
   Roll 'em over on their backs,
   They provide my little snacks,
   I'm a jumbuck skinning man.

3. Takes me rope when first I spies 'em,
   Catches 'em and then I rides 'em,
   Rides 'em, ties 'em, then I fries 'em,
   I'm a jumbuck skinning man.

jumbuck—sheep

'Waltzing Matilda' is not the only Australian song. This one comes from New South Wales, and is based on an unusual five-note scale. Sing it with tremendous vitality.

Time for Man Go Home Pupils' Book pp. 54 & 55

Trinidad Song

Slow

Time for man go home, Time for man go home.

Time for man go home, Time for man go home.____

It's time for man and it's time for beast, Time for man go home.____

De bird 'n de bush bawl 'kwa, kwa, kwa!' Time for man go home.____

Bu-cra bring old i-ron to break a man down, Time for man go home.____

De mon-key a-bush bawl 'kwa, kwa, kwa!' Time for man go home.

Time for man go home, Time for man go home.

Time for man go home, Time for man go home.

This is a work song, sung at the end of the day; the singers are tired, but their master ('bucra') makes them go on working. Quiet singing is needed, but the words must be clear and the pitch true. The song has been arranged for three unaccompanied voices, but don't let this frighten you; it is not nearly so difficult as it may look at first sight.

First sing the solos yourself, leaving the children to sing the top notes of the choruses except in the last two bars when they must sing the 'middle' notes. They will notice almost at once that in fact they have only two different phrases to sing, both of them very easy. Now ask them to sing the lower chorus notes, the ones with their stems going down; again there are only two different patterns to remember, both of them simple. Finally (but not all in one lesson!) try both parts together. The solo phrases can, if you prefer it, be sung by a small group.

Slowness of movement, slowness of speech: both are explored in ideas on these last pages.

By The Stream

Pupils' Book p. 57

One Man Shall Mow My Meadow   Pupils' Book p. 58

English Folk-Song

(And so on.)

The repeated bar must be sung twice in verse 2, three times in verse 3, and so on. Do not take this song too fast. If you sing it through to yourself, you will find that the semi-quavers in bar 3 indicate the right speed.

Manamolela

Pupils' Book pp. 60 & 61

Bantu Work Song

Translated by Pete Seeger

Like 'Time for Man Go Home', this is a work song for singers who are tired, and for that reason it should not be taken too fast. The work that they are doing is hoeing in the fields. As with so many African songs, the rise and fall of the tune roughly follows the rise and fall of the words when spoken, and we cannot hope to achieve authenticity with an English translation; nevertheless we can still derive a great deal of interest and pleasure from songs like this one.

The top stave makes a perfectly satisfactory unison song, and in any case it should first be taught on its own. When you come to look at the lower stave you will see that it is for the most part a repetition of the top one.

You may find an echo of the two-part 'Manamolela' in the picture (Pupils' Book p. 59), by the way in which the figures are grouped.

Sweet Polly Oliver

Pupils' Book p. 62

English Traditional Song

1. As sweet Pol-ly O-li-ver lay mu-sing in bed,
2. So ear-ly next morn-ing she soft-ly a-rose,

A sud-den strange fan-cy came in-to her head;
And dressed her-self up in her dead bro-ther's clothes;

'Nor fa-ther nor mo-ther shall make me false prove!
She cut her hair close and she stained her face brown,

I'll 'list for a sol-dier and fol-low my love!'
And went for a sol-dier to fair Lon-don town.

3. Then up spoke the sergeant one day at his drill:
   'Now who's good for nursing? A captain lies ill!'
   'I'm ready,' says Polly; to nurse him she's gone,
   And finds 'tis her true love all wasted and wan.

4. The first week the doctor kept shaking his head;
   'No nursing, young fellow, can save him,' he said.
   But when Polly Oliver had nursed back his life,
   He cried, 'You have cherished him as if you were his wife!'

5. Oh then Polly Oliver she burst into tears,
   And told the good doctor her hopes and her fears.
   And very soon after, for better or for worse,
   The captain took joyfully his pretty soldier nurse.

The accompaniment is sufficient as it stands, but if you wish you can fill in the chords to give a fuller sound. Explain the meaning of 'musing' and 'enlist' in verse 1.

We began these books with a song about the seasons. We finish with a poem by a class of second-year juniors about the same subject (Pupils' Book p. 63).

Goodbye Winter, Hello Spring!
Winter was cold and the trees were dead;
Bored with Winter's long black nights,
I like to see Spring's sparkling lights.

The air is fresh and clean and clear;
The sun frees green leaves from their cells,
And birds build nests to lay their eggs,
And young lambs tremble on new legs.

Spring is short and quickly goes;
Alas, the animals have grown.
Confetti blossom falls like rain;
Spring has gone, it's Summer again.

Examine this poem, or better still one written by your own class, for its possibilities of sound illustration; the sounds could be a background to the words or interludes between verses. Use the words for choral speech, breaking them up and allocating them to single voices, groups, the entire class. Can any words be used as an ostinato accompaniment? Do any of them suggest rhythms which might be clapped?

Once the poem has been explored in these ways, turn from the words themselves to the ideas they express. The seasons make a pattern of growth, decay, and re-birth. A group composition on this theme would be very rewarding.

Recalling the way you may have composed instrumental pieces earlier in the book, now work with the children either as a class or in groups on a piece about the seasons. With the poem and this piece, and with the possible addition of recorder tunes and songs, you should make a very lively and varied sequence to appeal to the ear.

But do not forget the eye. If you can find an opportunity for movement and if you can provide pictures, plants, and other materials, you will enrich the whole undertaking.

APPENDIX 1
Hand Signs

te

lah

soh

fah 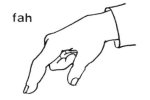 OR fah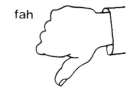

me

ray

doh

APPENDIX 2
Alternative Accompaniments

We have written special accompaniments for most of the songs, but in many cases it is possible to play on a guitar much simpler accompaniments based on only two or three chords. We give below a list of songs which can be accompanied in this way. These chords cannot be used at the same time as the written accompaniments.

Two-chord songs (I—tonic (doh), V—dominant (soh))

Seasons	Nine Red Horsemen
The Spinning Song	Bought Me a Cat
Down by the Crystal Fountain	Spring Carol
Down in Demerara	Sourwood Mountain
Bobby Shaftoe	

Three-chord songs (I—tonic (doh), IV—subdominant (fah), V—dominant (soh))

Who's Dat Yonder?	Kumba Yah
The Four Farmers	This Old Man
Mister Rabbit	Leave Her, Johnny
Venezuelan Carol	The Girl Who Liked Dancing
The Holy Child	The Birds' Wedding
Go and Tell Aunt Nancy	The Riddle
The Little Pig	Sweet Nightingale
Sing, Said the Mother	Hill an' Gully
Michael Finnigin	When I First Came to This Land

APPENDIX 3
The Tape

A tape has been prepared for use with these books; it contains all the short extracts of recorded music mentioned at intervals throughout the Teacher's Manual. These pieces are listed below with the appropriate page reference numbers. Since counting mechanisms vary on different tape recorders, numbers for tape reference are not given. The music has been recorded at a speed of $3\frac{3}{4}$ i.p.s. mono; it is also available as a stereo cassette.

The tape contains the following music:

1. Marais: *Le Basque* (p. 47)
2. Rossini: Storm Music, from overture to *William Tell* (p. 49)
3. Salzedo: *Son* (p. 60)
4. Spanish Dance: *Pandeirada* (p. 60)
5. Ravel: 'Hop o' My Thumb', from *Ma Mère L'Oye* (p. 65)
6. Salzedo: *Ritmos* (p. 84)
7. Orff: Extract from *Music for Children* (p. 108)
8. Rossini: 'Tarantella', arr. Respighi, from *La Boutique Fantasque* (p. 123)
9. Bizet: 'Carillon', from *L'Arlésienne* (p. 131)
10. Vaughan Williams: 'March', from *Folk Song Suite* (p. 145)
11. Messaien: 'Epôde', from *Chronochromie* (p. 155)
12. Milhaud: *Le Coucou* (p. 155)

If further recorded music is needed at this stage, the record *Tunes for Children*, HMV 7EG 8575 issued to accompany the original Junior Series, will be found useful. It contains arrangements of a number of short pieces by various composers, with arrangements of folk-songs and dances. These will provide extra material for listening, for movement, and for composition.

APPENDIX 4

Care of Equipment

If the equipment used in music lessons is to give the best service possible it must be carefully kept in good working condition. Unless you are an expert, do not attempt any major repairs yourself: breakages should be reported immediately to the specialists employed by the local education authority. But there are certain things for which you must be responsible.

The Piano

Make sure that the piano is tuned regularly and keep a record of any mechanical defects to give to the tuner on his next visit. The instrument should stand away from radiators or other sources of heat, and there should always be humidifiers in centrally-heated rooms where the atmosphere is likely to get very dry; at the opposite extreme, avoid excessive dampness. One of the worst enemies of all instruments is dust, and in the classroom you will need to keep a duster handy. From time to time the keys should be cleaned with a moistened cloth. When the piano is not in regular use, it is advisable to protect it with a cloth cover; with the children's help this can be made to look gay and attractive.

The Gramophone and Records

The maintenance and servicing of the gramophone may not be your responsibility, but at least make sure that it is not placed near a radiator or other source of heat, and watch out for dust. When this gets inside the machine it can be blown out by a photographic 'blow brush'. Dust and fluff also accumulate round the stylus and must be removed with a small brush specially made for the purpose. A 'dust-bug' fitted to the turntable helps to remove dust from the record as it is being played, and reduces static. This prolongs the record's life. The piece of equipment that often receives least attention, and yet can do most damage to records, is the stylus itself. A stylus is designed to be used only so much, the number of times depending on whether it is a sapphire or a diamond. In order to keep a check on its use it is worth buying a special disc check counter. When a record is not in use it should be stored well away from sources of heat, in an upright position, to prevent warping. When it is taken out of the bag it should be handled by its edge to avoid damage to the surface, and the effects of moisture from the hands. Various specially prepared disc-cleaning cloths are now available.

The Tape Recorder and Tapes

Dust and dirt are also enemies of the tape recorder, which should be kept well covered when not in use. The faces of the heads are best cleaned with an ordinary stencil brush dipped in a little methylated spirits. The tapes should be kept in a soft polythene bag inside a cardboard or metal container in an upright position and with the name of the recording clearly marked on the container. They, too, should be stored in a place without extremes of temperature and away from magnetic fields. It is wise to rewind each tape every two years; for this, specialist help may be needed.

Purchase of equipment

A series of specifications and purchasing recommendations for musical equipment, including electronic equipment, has been prepared by the British Standards Institution, British Standards House, 2 Park Street, London W.1. Amongst these is a useful pamphlet on 'How to look after a piano' (P.D. 5273), and another for schools with string classes, 'Care and Maintenance of Stringed Instruments' (P.D. 5286); see also *Basic String Repairs* by Arthur Burgan (OUP, London, 1974).

APPENDIX 5

Songs Graded for Reading

Book 1

PITCH

The intervals in this book to which attention is drawn cover the complete major scale, the major common chord and the pentatonic scale. Some of them are given in both ascending and descending form: in a few of the songs they can be found in both these forms.

Stepwise

d r	'The Four Farmers' (p. 46); 'The Walnut Tree' (p. 92)
d r m	'Seasons' (p. 39); 'The Spinning Song' (p. 42); 'Khasi's Lullaby' (p. 44); 'The Baby King' (p. 58)
(m r d)	'Who's Dat Yonder?' (p. 40);' Go and Tell Aunt Nancy' (p. 69)
d r m f s	'Unto Us a Boy is Born' (p. 54); 'Down in Demerara' (p. 66); 'This Old Man' (p. 83)
(s f m r d)	'The Baby King' (p. 58); 'My Goose' (p. 68); 'Birthday Round' (p. 98)
s l t d'	'Unto Us a Boy is Born' (p. 54);
s₁ l t d	'The Girl Who Liked Dancing' (p. 105)
d' t l s f m r d	'Pirulito' (p. 102)

(particularly useful for stepwise revision is 'Nine Red Horsemen' (p. 86) which ends with these phrases: m' r' d' t l s f; r' d' t l s f m;
d' t' l s f m r; t l s f m r d.)

Chordal

d m	'Down by the Crystal Fountain' (p. 48); 'The Holy Child' (p. 62); 'The Walnut Tree' (p. 92)
(m d)	'Seasons' (p. 39); 'Who's Dat Yonder?' (p. 40); 'The Spinning Song' (p. 42); 'The Four Farmers' (p. 46)
d s	'We Wish You a Merry Christmas' (p. 60); 'The Walnut Tree' (p. 92)
(s d)	'This Old Man' (p. 83); 'The Walnut Tree' (p. 92); 'Post-horn Signal' (p. 108)
m s	'Khasi's Lullaby' (p. 44); 'Mister Rabbit' (p. 52); 'The Baby King' (p. 58); 'The Little Pig' (p. 70)
(s m)	'Sing, Said the Mother' (p. 72); 'This Old Man' (p. 83); 'The Walnut Tree' (p. 92); 'Post-horn Signal' (p. 108)
d m s	'Rocking' (p. 56); 'Kumba Yah' (p. 78); 'There's a Young Lad' (p. 78); 'Turn the Glasses Over' (p. 81); 'Bought Me a Cat' (p. 88); 'Leave Her, Johnny' (p. 94)
(s m d)	'Mister Rabbit' (p. 52); 'Bobby Shaftoe' (p. 74)
s₁ d	'Mister Rabbit' (p. 52); 'The Holy Child' (p. 62); 'Down in Demerara' (p. 66); 'Michael Finnigin' (p. 76); 'The Girl Who Liked Dancing' (p. 105);
(d s₁)	'The Spinning Song' (p. 42)
m s₁	'Post-horn Signal' (p. 108)
s₁ s	'We Wish You a Merry Christmas' (p. 60)
d d'	'There's a Young Lad' (p. 78)
d' m	'There's a Young Lad' (p. 78)

Pentatonic Scale

d r m s l	'Mister Rabbit' (p. 52); 'The Swapping Song' (p. 100); 'Leave Her, Johnny' (p. 94)

Two other useful intervals

d f	'Bobby Shaftoe' (p. 74); 'The Walnut Tree' (p. 92)
d l	'Venezuelan Carol' (p. 59)

RHYTHM

In Book 1 the concentration is on rhythmic elements from Simple Time. The titles in italics are tunes.

♪♪♩ 'Seasons' (p. 39); 'The Spinning Song' (p. 42); 'The Four Farmers' (p. 46); 'Michael Finnigin' (p. 76); *'Hungarian Folk-Song'* (p. 82); *'Pavane'* (p. 102); *'The Cobbler's Jig'* (p. 106)

♩ ♪♪ 'Down by the Crystal Fountain' (p. 48); 'The Holy Child' (p. 62); 'Down in Demerara' (p. 66); 'My Goose' (p. 68); *'Chong Chong Nai'* (p. 40); *'Dance Tune'* (p. 50); *'Egyptian Folk Tune'* (p. 87); *'Spanish Dance Tune'* (p. 104)

♪♪♪ or ♪♪♪♪ 'Down by the Crystal Fountain' (p. 48); 'The Little Pig' (p. 70); 'Sing, Said the Mother' (p. 72); 'Bobby Shaftoe' (p. 74); *'Hungarian Folk Tune'* (p. 51); *'Hungarian Folk-Song'* (p. 82); *'Spanish Dance Tune'* (p. 104); *'The Cobbler's Jig'* (p. 106)

𝄾 ♪ 'Mister Rabbit' (p. 52); 'The Little Pig' (p. 70); 'The Donkey's Burial' (p. 90)

♩ 'Unto Us a Boy is Born' (p. 54); 'Rocking' (p. 56); *'Dodo, l'Enfant Do'* (p. 55); *'Gaelic Lullaby'* (p. 65); *'Pavane'* (p. 102)

♩. 'Venezuelan Carol' (p. 59); *'Pant Corlan Yr Wyn'* (p. 80)

♩. ♪ 'Bought Me a Cat' (p. 88); 'The Donkey's Burial' (p. 90); 'Leave Her, Johnny' (p. 94); 'The Mocking Bird' (p. 107); *'Chong Chong Nai'* (p. 40); *'Egyptian Folk Tune'* (p. 87); *'Spanish Dance Tune'* (p. 104)

♪♪♪ 'Down by the Crystal Fountain' (p. 48)

Book 2

PITCH

All the intervals to which attention was drawn in Book 1 will also be found in this book. New intervals to notice are:

d' l or d l₁	'The Riddle' (p. 114); 'Soldier, Soldier' (p. 117); 'Past Three O'Clock' (p. 130)
(l d')	'The Keeper' (p. 138)
r f	'The Birds' Wedding' (p. 110); 'Sweet Nightingale' (p. 140)
(f r)	'The Birds' Wedding' (p. 110); 'Old Aunt Kate' (p. 112); 'The Grey Hawk' (p. 154); 'Eastertide' (p. 158); 'Time for Man Go Home' (p. 170)
r s	'The Birds' Wedding' (p. 110); 'The Old Man of the Woods' (p. 124); 'Eastertide' (p. 158)
(s r)	'Past Three O'Clock' (p. 130)
r s₁	'Sweet Nightingale' (p. 140); 'The Grey Hawk' (p. 154)
r l₁	'Spring Carol' (p. 159)
r l₁	'Eastertide' (p. 158); 'The Grey Hawk' (p. 154)
r t₁	'The Birds' Wedding' (p. 110); 'When I First Came to this Land' (p. 150)
m l	'Past Three O'Clock' (p. 130)
(l m)	'Sourwood Mountain' (p. 160)
m l₁	'The Holly and the Ivy' (p. 122); 'John Barleycorn' (p. 146)
f l	'The Little Dove' (p. 120)
(l f)	'The Riddle' (p. 114); 'The Grey Hawk' (p. 154)
s s'	'The Grey Hawk' (p. 154); 'Eastertide' (p. 158)
(s' s)	'The Birds' Wedding' (p. 110)
s t	'Children Go, I Will Send You' (p. 126)
(t s)	'The Little Dove' (p. 120); 'Sweet Polly Oliver' (p. 176)

188

RHYTHM

Rhythmic elements to notice:

Simple Time

'The Birds' Wedding' (p. 110); 'Soldier, Soldier' (p. 117);

'To Bethlehem' (p. 128); 'Manamolela' (p. 174)

'Old Aunt Kate' (p. 112); 'To Bethlehem' (p. 128)
'Old Aunt Kate' (p. 112); 'The Riddle' (p. 114);
'Kukuriku' (p. 118); 'Sur Le Pont d'Avignon' (p. 134);
'Manamolela' (p. 174)

'Past Three O'Clock' (p. 130)

Compound Time

All the songs in ⁶⁄₈. (The more difficult groups in
'Heave Away' (p. 152) and 'One Man Shall Mow My Meadow'
(p. 173) need not be used for reading purposes at this stage)

'The Farmer's Daughter' (p. 116);
'The Wee Cooper O' Fife' (p. 162)

Make a point of revising ♩. ♪ in the following songs:

'The Keeper' (p. 138); 'Sweet Nightingale' (p. 140); 'High Germany' (p. 144);
'John Barleycorn' (p. 146); 'When I First Came to this Land' (p. 150);
'Hark, the Bells' (p. 156); 'Spring Carol' (p. 159); 'Hush-You-Bye' (p. 164);
'Jumbuck Skinning Man' (p. 168).

The recorder melodies in Book 2 revise the rhythmic elements already introduced in Book 1

Index